BEL**i**EVE

A Confrontation with Christianity's
Biggest Challenges

PETER HECK

Library of Congress Cataloging-in-Publication Data

ISBN-13: 978-1479274130
ISBN-10: 1479274135

Published in the United States by
Attaboy Press

a division of Attaboy Productions, Inc.
2004 Waverly Drive
Kokomo, IN 46902

For more information on Attaboy Productions, Inc., please visit:
www.peterheck.com/peterheck/attaboy

Distributed in cooperation with
CreateSpace
7290 B. Investment Drive
Charleston, SC 29418

SMALL GROUP STUDY CURRICULUM

ORDER RIGHT NOW

NINE POWERFUL DVD SESSIONS!

INDIVIDUAL STUDY GUIDE BOOKLETS!

PROVOCATIVE DISCUSSION STARTERS!

"ALWAYS BE PREPARED TO GIVE AN ANSWER TO ANYONE WHO ASKS YOU TO GIVE A REASON FOR THE HOPE THAT YOU HAVE."

2 Peter 3:15

Customized orders to fit the size of your Sunday School class, Small Group, Community Group or family...

Order online at: www.peterheck.com/believe

Or by calling: 765-450-5220

To Addie and Bristol.

There's nothing I pray for more than to watch you both grow into loving, courageous and committed champions for Jesus.

CONTENTS

Introduction

(YES, YOU SHOULD READ THIS)

I should have probably made these brief comments Chapter One of the book rather than the Introduction, because I'm afraid too many people are like me. Whenever I pick up a book to read, I almost always skip the Preface or Introduction and dig into the text. Because after all, there's something psychologically demoralizing about having read a book for 20 minutes, only to have to put it down, short of page one. There's simply no sense of satisfaction when someone asks you how far you made it and you have to tell them, "Oh, I think I'm on page vii."

Still, the logistics of this book forced my hand. Since we're tackling nine of the big challenges to the Christian faith, I just couldn't see putting you, the reader, through the confusion of challenge one being in Chapter Two, challenge two being in Chapter Three, and so on. See my dilemma? So here it is...an

Introduction. But for those who are actually reading this, I'm at least going to do two things to make it less obnoxious. First, I'll keep it short. And second, no Roman Numerals. Please note the actual page number above – you are accomplishing something as you read this.

The reason I wrote this book is quite simple. For several years now, whether through my radio show, speaking engagements or written commentaries, I have spent a lot of time talking and arguing with people about politics and the direction of American society. And while my convictions have not changed, nor have my beliefs that such work is vital to turning around the cultural decay that threatens our civilization, I have developed a better and wiser understanding of the reasons for our disagreements: we aren't starting from the same foundation point.

If God did not exist, I would probably not have the same view on abortion as I do. If the Bible were not God's own revealed Word of Truth to mankind, I would certainly have a different take on homosexuality. What that means is that it is highly unlikely I'm going to make any progress in changing someone else's mind on an issue if we hold two completely different sets of presuppositions. In other words, rather than growing frustrated at seemingly futile arguments over the manifestations of our beliefs, we would be wise to concentrate on determining whose beliefs are better – or at least who has the more reliable foundation for their beliefs.

And when we Christians do that, all of a sudden we begin to see our adversaries not as enemies, but as captives; captives to a warped foolishness that rejects the sovereignty of God and replaces it with the subjective whims of humanity. Yet with as backwards and dangerous as it may be, that humanist ideology is becoming an increasingly formidable force in America, making more profound inroads into the collective conscious of each successive generation. The dumbing down of the American mind, all while puffing out our chests in the name of intellectualism, has rendered even lifelong churchgoers susceptible to the deceit.

That is the point of this book and the entire BELiEVE project, which includes an interactive video series with study guides for Sunday School classes, small groups and families, online resources at www.peterheck.com/believe, and live multimedia speaking presentations.

Now, if you're tempted to think, "Taking on challenges to Christianity isn't exactly an original or novel concept," you're right. And that's one of the most important things I wanted to stress in this Introduction. Ecclesiastes 1:9 tells us that, "What has been will be again, what has been done will be done again; there is nothing new under the sun," and that's certainly true for the Christian apologetics you will read in this book. What follows is a compilation of some of the great research and work that has been done through the years by Biblical scholars and philosophers, deep thinkers and men and women far more intelligent than I – and maybe you – could ever hope to be.

In other words, these pages are not filled with my own wisdom or insight. What I have attempted to do is to take the brilliant intuitions and ponderings of these great minds and transmit them or teach them in an understandable, concise, entertaining, and hopefully new way.

With the extraordinarily heavy subject matter we are engaging, you will find these chapters to be tremendously short. Editing and paring down so many great observations, points and truths was without question the hardest part of this project. But given the reality that we live in a fast-food, sensory-overload culture, where attention spans run shorter than ever, I wanted to find a way to address these grand dilemmas and debates simply and directly.

Some will undoubtedly criticize this approach, claiming that I am short-changing the serious nature of these issues by not writing volumes on each. I couldn't disagree more. What truly short-changes the seriousness of these topics is a willingness to let the vast majority of men who will never pick up a 1,000 page dissertation on each, continue stumbling around in the darkness. I believe it is the challenge of our time to find ways to educate ourselves – as well as the minds of others – with the ancient truths of God's revelation in a manner and mode that isn't ancient.

Still, some of you may feel like even in these

shorter chapters you are drinking from a fire hose. I pray that you will diligently take the time to go back through the material and grasp it all. Highlight and commit these points to memory. Because as our culture turns increasingly post-Christian, these are the challenges that will be posed in an effort to keep others from a relationship with God. We must be prepared with an answer.

Others of you will probably feel like I'm just getting started when the chapter ends. You will crave more. You will want something deeper, heavier, more heady and intellectual. Find it. Literally thousands of volumes have been written on many of these topics. Please don't consider what I cover in the following pages all there is to say on the subject. I encourage you to better equip yourself, enrich yourself, empower yourself with the truth. It is that alone which will set the captives free.

Scientists like Ken Ham and his team at Answers in Genesis boast an incredibly state-of-the-art website (www.answersingenesis.org), which hosts thousands of scholarly articles that will educate you. Biblical thinkers like Glenn Miller and his online Christian Think Tank (www.christianthinktank.com) dive into some of the most philosophically perplexing questions of the faith. C.S. Lewis, R.C. Sproul, Augustine of Hippo, Martin Luther, Francis Schaeffer, G.K. Chesterton, Ravi Zacharias, Josh McDowell and so many others offer thousands, if not millions of pages that provide deep, unmistakable evidence for the truth of the Christian revelation.

Their work has inspired me and provided me with the answers I sought to embolden my faith and strengthen my convictions. It is my prayer that this book will either begin, or further that same process for you…and that you would emerge a more confident, a more committed, a more courageous disciple of Jesus, the Christ.

Okay, you've made it to Chapter One now…

1

"THERE IS NO GOD"

The Challenge

If you were a servant in a warm castle in dead of winter, and I a freezing traveler in the snow outside your doorstop, you might invite me in to warm myself by the fire in an inner room. But I, looking through your open doorway, would see no fire, but only the fireless outer room, and I would have to trust your promise that I could get warm 'if I only stepped inside', judging the legitimacy of that promise on the basis of characteristics about you--the fact that you were not dressed heavily for the cold, that your hands actually felt warm, that you SEEMED to radiate honesty, and that you could make descriptive statements about the fire. If I insisted that I would not take that first step into the castle until I could actually SEE the fire in the inner room, I would obviously have to stay in the cold...

Of course, if your hands were COLD instead of warm, you were shivering, and you were dressed in heaviest furs, I would suspect duplicity, and be wise to take my chances with the snow and wolves, than with a fellow human with dishonesty in his heart, leading me into who-knows-what treachery...

I feel a little like the servant in that story...I am very, very warmed by the Fire but am limited to sharing the warmth of my hands, my 'non-verbal' expressions, the way I dress, and the grossly insufficient language to describe such a robust thing as a fire...

You may decide that my hands might not be warm enough to provide evidence for the existence of the Fire, or that my manner of dealing with 'questions' and/or 'people' might not be honest or 'objective,' or that my manner of arranging my life reveals that I really DON'T believe there's a Fire warming me.

But what else can I do?[1]   *- Glenn Miller*

Skeptics and Scoffers

A few years ago, I shared with the audience of my radio program the most bizarre – and yet unquestionably entertaining – email I have ever received from someone who disagrees with me. Responding to a segment I aired that was apparently far too evangelistic for his taste, a man named Terry wrote,

"I've had it with your incessant Bible banging. You seem to be an intelligent person, but just when I'm beginning to give you credit for being educated, you start talking about God and totally blow it. How much more evidence do you need to see around you to recognize that there is no God? Can you prove Him? Then do it. If not, accept the fact that He's not there and quit trying to fool others. What a waste you make of your time and your life when you talk about God. How pathetic for you that when you get to the end of your life and there is no God waiting for you, there you will be, staring out into the cosmic nothingness and the abyss that is eternity wondering where He is. And I will be there. Laughing at you."

Call it twisted, but the mere thought of our two beleaguered souls dangling in the darkness over an inexhaustible abyss, with the everlasting silence of "cosmic nothingness" pierced only by his uproarious laughter over how wrong I was about God just cracks me up. Under what delusion must you put yourself to think that in such a hopeless state you could find the desire to condescendingly mock another?

But you need not be a radio talk show host to have experienced similar taunts, even if less dramatic. Any Christian who doesn't live in a cave, isolated from humanity and internet access, has undoubtedly been confronted by a non-believer who militantly states their position that, "There is no God." They take great pride in challenging us Christians to "prove" God. After all, they reason, if He does exist, He should be easy to prove.

Sometimes their questions are sincere, while other times they are tinged with taunts and self-righteousness. For our own sanity, it's critical that we be able to distinguish the difference. Many skeptics do ultimately seek truth – they want answers. But, as hard as it is to believe or as difficult as it is to swallow, the reality is that there are those who simply seek to antagonize. They don't want answers from us because they're convinced they already have them – and the answers they have come to don't include any God.

These are the Starbucks philosophers. The ones who take great pride in their own intellect and invite you for a cup of coffee just so they can impress upon you how profound their thinking is. Many times they will invite others as well, in an attempt to demonstrate the deep reasoning they are capable of performing in comparison to the mindless crutch that religion provides unseasoned thinkers like you. Regardless of how effectively you answer their questions, they have three more to fire at you – each becoming more obscure, confused and convoluted. The more complex and strained their long-winded questions and pontifications become, the less you are able to even attempt a response, primarily because you aren't even sure there's a question to respond to. And each time you can't respond – or don't – they take that as a victory, notching up another win for "rational

thinking" over religious fantasy. If you pay close
attention you will notice that they don't even seem to
be listening to what you're saying in response, but
rather positioning themselves for the next argument.

The truth is that these antagonists really
shouldn't be termed skeptics because they aren't. A
true skeptic is one who, though he has doubts, leaves
his mind open to possibilities he might not be overly
comfortable with believing. In other words, a true
skeptic doesn't enter into the pursuit of truth with a
pre-determined conclusion in mind. Those who do are
better termed scoffers; scoffers whose hearts are
rebellious to God.

The reason I mention this is, well, Facebook.
Kinda. Facebook is just the current outlet for the kinds
of inane discussions and "debates" that have tortured
believers for years. These exchanges really amount to
nothing more than prideful posturing that typically
hurt feelings, strain relationships and accomplish little.
Yet several Christians I know spend an inordinate
amount of time and energy trying to have rational and
reasoned discussions with scoffers who are simply
uninterested in listening. In other words, these well
intentioned believers waste their time dealing with
people that for whatever reason have built up a
calloused exterior that has to first be softened with acts
that are not intellectual or philosophical before any real
discussion can take place.

Until that occurs, as harsh as this may sound, the
hard hearts we encounter sometimes require the

shaking of dust from our sandals,[2] and the refusal to cast our pearls before swine.[3] Failing to recognize this Scriptural truth has caused many Christians serious migraines and an overabundance of unnecessary stress.

But for those who truly do seek truth, we would be very wise to establish at the outset of this monumentally big question of whether there is a God, that contrary to conventional wisdom, this is not a scientific question.

That's not to say that science won't play a part of the discussion or be involved in any conclusion we draw. It will. If God exists, science should testify to that truth. But alone, science is not a field capable of providing an answer to our dilemma.

Why? Well, science tells us about the physical world around us. We can run experiments, tests, have hypotheses that we confirm or reject about various phenomena. But this question of whether there is a God is a question about whether there is something beyond the physical world – something that started this physical world – that exists outside of the physical laws that we study in science.

At its heart, then, this is a philosophical question. Biology, cosmology, history, archaeology, experience, sociology, psychology – they will all inform the discussion, and collectively can point us in the direction of a conclusion, but ultimately they are at best going to be witnesses to the answer, not capable of providing an answer alone.

Now, some haughty skeptics will take that admission as an opportunity to sneer, "So you're saying you can't prove God?!" Well, yes, they're right. We can't. But intellectual honesty on their part or ours would demand us to realize that fact is precisely what we should expect if in fact there is a God.

Logically, it wouldn't even make sense to say you could "prove God."

Think about it this way. My oldest daughter, Addie, is obsessed with inflatable plastic kickballs. She can't get enough of them. It's so bad that we have to purposely avoid the three grocery store aisles closest to the ball cage because she can sense that she's getting close and a fit ensues. Unfortunately, I don't always remember that, and as a consequence our living room constantly has anywhere from five to six of those dumb things laying around just begging for me to step on them at night and break my ankle. Anyway, picture one of those plastic kickballs in your mind and imagine that it represented the world. Inside that ball were all the physical laws of the universe functioning perfectly, exactly as I - the ball designer - had created them. Given that scenario, the question we are asking is whether I exist - a being beyond the boundaries of that ball.

The laws of science that exist within the parameters of that ball - laws that I created - would logically bear evidence of my handiwork, but would be incapable of encapsulating or defining me. I would not be subject to the laws that I created as I would exist outside of them. Therefore, any argument that says "God can't exist because He would shatter everything we know about science – He wouldn't be bound by gravity or the laws of momentum or volition" is just silly.

If there is a God, He would have to be greater and beyond those laws. He would have to be greater and beyond our scope or complete understanding, otherwise He wouldn't be God. A human who claims to be capable of defining or putting definitive boundaries around what and who God is, isn't claiming to prove God. He's claiming to be God.

So the best answer to a skeptic who says, "You can't use science to prove God" is to look at them and say, "Precisely. And that very fact is proof itself." They will love that.

This reality that our finite minds cannot prove an infinite God doesn't mean that the question is pointless or unworthy of our time and study. Remember, just because we can't definitely prove God or disprove Him, we should be able to see His fingerprints if He is there. So let's dive into this philosophical question, understanding that if there is a God of truth, He is not afraid of our questions.[4]

The Testimony of the Human Race

One of the most profound, but often overlooked peculiarities about this question is the fact that a belief in something beyond our physical, human existence has been embraced by a near unanimity of the human race. Think about that. Nothing else comes close to having that kind of universal support.

Think of how powerful of evidence, how amazing of a fingerprint that truly is: crossing cultures, languages, beliefs, customs, traditions, tribe, creed, age and gender is this human conviction that there is something or *Someone* beyond us. It's remarkable. Our earliest human records show cultures with well-defined religious beliefs. And while some skeptics will correctly argue that religious beliefs were used and exploited by kings and lords to convince the peasant people of their Divine Right to rule, historical fidelity requires they acknowledge that long before that method of exploitation arose, countless earthly rulers who possessed unimaginable power stood quaking, prostrate before their gods.[5]

Go back to humankind's earliest days, even before written accounts, and you see the same thing. Cave drawings, engravings, and depictions from prehistoric times reveal supernatural beings that were collectively feared. And that's not all. Ancient burial practices of various cultures, like the Great Pyramids, reveal the certainty of a belief in some afterlife. Don't be tempted to think that these were just some primitive systems of thought embraced by civilizations that rejected the sciences. To the contrary, the most technologically and scientifically advanced civilizations of every generation – including our own – have embraced the concept of a "beyond."

And notice also that even those intellectuals who boldly proclaim to reject the notion of God have found their way to mystical explanations for some greater force that is beyond us, that is guiding us and directing the natural laws that surround us.

Now, does all this prove that God exists? Does the overwhelming consensus of humanity make the belief true? No. It is possible – however inconceivable – that the near entirety of the human race has been utterly wrong on this question. I am not suggesting that we should simply take everybody else's word for it, or that we should follow the crowd into blind trust.

But I've heard it put another way that is worth pondering: if you're driving down a road and every other car you see is traveling in the opposite direction, on both sides of you, there's a very high degree of likelihood that you're going the wrong way down a one way street.[6] Maybe everyone else made the mistake and your car is the only right one on the road. But rational, reasoned thinking would suggest otherwise.

The most plausible explanation from a philosophical standpoint, then, is that something appears to have been hard-wired into humanity to believe in something "beyond."

The Testimony of First Cause

Some will argue that the idea that there is an eternal being who has always been, a Creator who was uncreated, a being that has "always been there" is silly. Perhaps. But have you paused to actually consider the alternative? That's an important question if we're going to discuss silly ideas.

The alternative would be an infinite, unending history of causes and effects with nothing having ever started it – a long chain of dominoes that fall one after another, but no domino to ever start the chain. Or even more confounding: no being to put the dominoes in position.[7] Based on all human experience, such a concept seems far more unbelievable, problematic, and yes, silly, does it not?

Everything you have ever seen, touched or experienced has been an "effect" that was distinct and separate from, yet also the result of, some cause. Applying that experience to the universe then would make it far more logical to conclude that there was a *First Cause* to the world, life and the cosmos…something distinct from those things that caused them.

Interestingly, it's pretty telling to note that most of the leading non-theist, anti-Christian scientists will even admit the necessity of a *First Cause*. They usually attribute that cause to some kind of natural "singularity," but logically that's not possible. Why, you ask?

The Testimony of Complexity

Now, here's where it really gets fascinating. If

we keep following the laws of logic forward, accepting that there was some first cause to all things, we would have to conclude that whatever caused this universe would necessarily need to be at least as complex as the universe itself. Why is that? Well, a less complex *Beyond* or *First Cause* could not birth or design a more complex universe. The product could not – cannot – have more information or complexity than its source. Whatever started all this had to have as a part of it, at least as much of the information and complexity we now see around us, but probably more.

So then, it's helpful to try to think of the most complex entity that we know in our universe. Of all our discoveries and experiments, what is the most complex unit we can find? Would it not be the human spirit and personality? Think about it – it's hard to even name or identify what I'm addressing…it's that complex.

The human character, our soul or spirit, our personality is such a mystery. There are entire realms of science that dig into it, only to be mystified at all that goes into making it function. Personality is capable of beauty or ugliness, certainly. But more than behavior, it's capable of these things we call hopes, ambitions, and dreams. Think how incredibly complex that is to try to explain or even comprehend from a scientific perspective, and how distinct it is from any other living creature. This personality empowers emotions like fear and joy, grief and relief. Yet those emotions are not mere products of our biology. There's something more that goes into them. Our personality is amazingly diverse in appearance, aggressiveness, assertiveness, preferences, and desires. The more we think about it, the fewer objections we have to identifying it as the most complex entity we have ever found in our universe.[8]

What that reveals to us from a logical standpoint is nothing short of remarkable. We can know that the *First Cause* or *Beyond* that we are discussing is at least as personal, at least as "real" as we are. This is no longer some faceless, impersonal force buzzing in a mystical cloud somewhere in the cosmos. The *First Cause* must be astoundingly personal – capable of even keener emotions, passions, feelings and reactions than we can experience as the mere "effects." Don't miss that significant point. Our own personality is amazing evidence for the existence of a personal, emotional God.

Now, though we are following logical rules to arrive at our conclusions, it is only fair to note that there could and would be several objections that would be leveled along the way. The skeptic might make a great number of protests to what we're saying. But ironically, by doing so, they provide the best testimony yet for the existence of God.

The Testimony of Logic Itself

When waging arguments for or against the existence of God, we rely on the enduring laws of logic. They provide the basis of the human reason we use when we argue with one another about anything. No one has to learn how to argue and, for the most part, no one has to be told when arguments aren't credible or are based on faulty logic. For instance, we may call it by a fancy name, but did anyone have to teach you the Law of Non-Contradiction? That's the simple principle of logic that says both A and non-A can't be true at the same time. Or to put that in plain English, the dog can't be both alive and dead at the same time. Or maybe a better example would be to say that it can't be raining and not raining at the same time (understanding that those statements would be talking about the same time and place).

Now, it's certainly true that there are more complex rules of logic that an average person may not instinctively know. Still, in our arguments, we all – believers and unbelievers – rely on those laws of logic and (here's the really important part) assume that they will never change. We assume that there will never be a condition where A and non-A can both be true at the same time. That's just a basic assumption we make without even thinking about it. But how can we do that? How do we know these laws implicitly? And how do we know that they are constant and will never change?

As a Christian, that's a pretty easy question to answer. The Bible explains that God is consistent, constant, and unchanging, and therefore it would only make sense that the natural laws of His universe will be as well. God is non-contradictory, so His laws are non-contradictory. And since He is unchanging, His laws will not change either.[9]

But how do we humans instinctively rely on this truth, regardless of whether we believe in Him or not? How does a skeptic who doubts – or a scoffer who flagrantly refuses to even intellectually consider God's existence – automatically lean on the laws of logic to state their cases and make the astounding assumption that those laws will never change? Again, as a Christian, the Bible makes sense of that as well when it articulates that God created us in His image, and therefore wired such truth into us.

But suppose there was no God, and that all that we see around us is the result of some random explosion, rapid expansion or grand cosmic accident. How or why could logical reasoning be possible? If the human mind were merely the product of random mutations, where did this instinctive reliance on logical law come from? And how could we just assume that those laws are unchanging? If God does not exist, we should have no basis for logical reasoning at all. Or to paraphrase C.S. Lewis: if the universe has no meaning, we should never be able to figure out that it has no meaning.

The same is true of science. It also depends on the reality that the universe obeys orderly laws that will never change. But why would it or should it if the universe was merely the result of an accident? What would prevent these laws from "accidentally" changing again?

The very fact that we can study science based on unchanging laws of nature, or that we can argue in a logical debate about God based on unchanging laws of logic, is itself proof He must exist.

Perhaps one of the reasons Scripture admonishes that "The fool says in his heart 'There is no God,'"[10] is because the only way that fool can argue his case scientifically or logically is if God exists, and he is therefore wrong.

2

"EVOLUTION EXPLAINS IT BETTER"

The Challenge

The famous English apologist William Paley delivered this argument for a "Designer" for the universe:

> *"In crossing a heath, suppose I pitched my foot against a stone, and were asked how the stone came to be there; I might possibly answer, that, for anything I knew to the contrary, it had lain there forever: nor would it perhaps be very easy to show the absurdity of this answer.*
>
> *But suppose I had found a watch upon the ground, and it should be inquired how the watch happened to be in that place; I should hardly think of the answer I had before given, that for anything I knew, the watch might have*

always been there. (...)

*There must have existed, at some time, and at
some place or other, an artificer or artificers,
who formed [the watch] for the purpose which
we find it actually to answer; who
comprehended its construction, and designed its
use. (...)*

*Every indication of contrivance, every
manifestation of design, which existed in the
watch, exists in the works of nature; with the
difference, on the side of nature, of being greater
or more, and that in a degree which exceeds all
computation.[1]*

*Paley's suggestion is that just like a watch
necessitates a watchmaker, the grand design of our universe
necessitates a grand designer. But a watchmaker creates
watches with pre-existing materials. God is stated to create
from scratch. This difference renders the analogy weak.
Further, a watchmaker makes watches but nothing else. We
would not see a laptop and assume that the watchmaker was
the designer. This indicates that the argument suggests
multiple creators; one for each type of thing that exists.*

*Finally, the first part of Paley's argument says that
the watch stands out from randomness of nature because it is
ordered. The second part of the argument claims that the
universe is obviously not random, but is ordered. This makes
the entire argument inconsistent. A better explanation of the
universe can be found through natural, not supernatural
causes.[2] – Atheist Think Tank*

Silent Witness

The first four words of the Bible are incredibly instructive as we piece together this notion of God. "In the beginning, God."[3] There is absolutely no effort in Scripture to prove God's existence or to argue or suggest that God had a beginning. And if we are thinking, that shouldn't surprise us.

As we mentioned in chapter one, in order for God to be that *First Cause*, He must – logically speaking – be outside of time and space, distinct from those effects that He caused. And since such a Being exists outside of our physical realm, it's illogical to think we could use the laws of our physical realm to define Him, encapsulate Him, fully explain Him or prove Him. What we should be able to do, though, is to see evidence of His handiwork – evidence that would bear witness to His existence. Does that evidence exist in our world? As I make the case that it does, I'll follow the outline of scientists Ken Ham and Dr. Jason Lisle in their straightforward essay, "Is There Really a God?"

Evidence of Intelligence

If you really want to see an archaeologist excited, simply watch them uncover stone tools in some ancient cave. It's like winning the Super Bowl to these guys. But why? Because they're nerds? Of course. But also because stone tools can't form themselves based on natural processes. Their formation requires intelligent input. And so the scientists who discover them can know that they have stumbled across evidence of early human beings capable of that kind of design.

We experience that kind of discovery ourselves every day, even if we don't pause long enough to notice. No one would believe that the stones forming the Great Wall of China slowly emerged over time on their own, or that a giant cathedral formed after a marble mine gradually eroded due to precipitation.[4]

I remember seeing a scene from the comedy *My Fellow Americans* that involved a Dad explaining to his young son how the carvings on Mount Rushmore were "one of the world's great natural wonders." That kind of parenting almost deserves a call to Child Protective Services.

Speaking of parenting, as a young boy I remember going to the Air Force base to visit my Dad who was a pilot and ROTC instructor. We would walk around the tarmac and look at all the cool jets made up of all those amazingly intricate parts. And as I would watch the mechanics working on them, I remember thinking how brilliant the men who designed that incredible aircraft must have been. Even as a kid who didn't have a clue about propulsion, lift, or any of the incredibly complicated processes that go into making a plane fly, I never once had a thought in my mind that the object I was looking at began as a pile of metal scraps, wheels and rods that formed on their own over time.

That's precisely the argument that William Paley, the famous Anglican preacher, was making in his watchmaker parallel: the great design we see around us necessitates a greater Designer. Yet as logical as that seems, an ever-growing number of people (including many scientists), are challenging those who believe in a Designer, saying that the slow evolutionary process explains it all better. Are they right?

The Admission of Design

Believe it or not, the scientists who reject God still acknowledge that living things exhibit the evidence of design. Dr. Richard Dawkins, perhaps the world's most recognizable atheist, wrote in his book *The Blind Watchmaker*, "We have seen that living things are too improbable and too beautifully 'designed' to have come into existence by chance."[5]

He's right, of course. Consider the odds of amino acids – the building blocks of life – arising by chance into a workable set is less than 1 in 10 to the 40,000[th] power. Another way of saying that is "mathematically impossible." But if men like Dawkins acknowledge the obvious – that it couldn't have been chance that led to life on earth, but rather it had to be designed – yet they also reject God as the Designer, who do they put in His place?

Maybe instead of saying "who," we would be more accurate to say "what." Dawkins and his fellow Darwinists say life arose thanks to the "blind forces of physics," operating through mutation and natural selection. In other words, evolution is the Designer.

And there are a lot of folks that are gravitating towards that explanation. That doesn't change the reality that there are some big problems with it. Let's look at some of them.

Problem One: "It's the Information, Stupid"

Life is built on information. The DNA code – which makes up the genes of any organism – is simply loaded with all kinds of specific, detailed and patterned material. That alone should be enough to point us in the direction of an intelligent agency. Consider that all human experience tells us that a pattern always indicates intelligence, not chance. When we listen intently into the galaxy for signs of intelligent life beyond our planet, what are we attempting to discern? A pattern amidst the noise of space. And why? Because a pattern would require the input of an intelligent source.

But beyond just that, have you paused to ask yourself where all those codes inside our DNA came from in the first place? The Biblical model says that a super-intelligent God put that information into creation. This, as we've said, is consistent with human experience. For instance, a computer program is equipped with loads of data, and it's there because an intelligent programmer put it there.

But remember that the evolutionary process begins with a single cell organism – something less complex than us – and says that over some 4.6 billion years (give or take…what's a few billion?), it evolved into something more complex. But that presents a pretty significant problem.

Maybe instead of thinking about DNA, using something more common to us like an encyclopedia might be helpful. Yes, I know they are now considered ancient, so stop laughing at the fact that I just said an encyclopedia is "common," and just go with it. The encyclopedia for a human contains a lot different and a lot more material than does an encyclopedia for the amoeba. So the question becomes, if we evolved from creatures like amoebas, where did all that new information come from in the process of our evolution?

Some evolutionists might suggest natural selection or adaptation.[6] But that can't possibly explain it. Think of how natural selection (or adaptation) has worked on developing the various breeds of dogs that we see – everything from wolves, coyotes and dingoes, all the way to poodles and labs. Over time, natural selection has operated on those genes, rearranging them, separating them, isolating them, promoting various kinds of information that was already within that dog breed to help it adapt to its surroundings and environment.

But notice in that example that no new data was added. And that reality is replicated everywhere we see natural selection at work. The process operates only on information already present, never contributing new information to the equation.

Honest evolutionists acknowledge this truth, but

they argue that gene mutations within the species produce the new information. They suggest that sometimes, while natural selection is working on the genes of a creature, a gene will mutate and will result in the emergence of new material.

While a nice thought, there's a pretty big problem with it. Dr. Lee Spetner explains it best:

> "In all the reading I've done in the life-sciences literature, I've never found a mutation that added information."

He goes on:

> "All point mutations that have been studied on the molecular level turn out to reduce the genetic information and not to increase it...Information cannot be built up by mutations that lose it. A business can't make money by losing it a little at a time...The failure to observe even one mutation that adds information is more than just a failure to find support for the theory (of evolution). It is evidence against the theory."[7]

Dr. Spetner's not alone. Dr. Werner Gitt confirms his conclusion,

> "Mutations can only cause changes in existing information. There can be no increase in information, and in general the results are injurious. New blueprints for new

functions or new organs cannot arise; mutations cannot be the source of new information."[8]

So if it's not natural selection – which only acts on existing information, and it can't be mutations – which always result in a loss of information…where did all this information come from?

Problem Two: "Speak the Language"

Many evolutionists like to try to skip that question and suggest that as long as somehow all the chemicals of life got together in one place, the information for life could have simply arisen by chance. They don't really know where it all came from, but they ignore that trivial question and say something like, "If all the chemicals were there together, it all could have happened by chance alone."

To picture how this would allegedly work, grab the closest book, hold it by its binding and dump all of its letters into a pot. Then pour all those letters out in a string on the floor. The evolutionist argument goes that if you start looking at that string of letters, you will find individual words that are spelled out like C-A-T or H-O-M-E. Those words, they point out, all emerged by chance. And their argument is that, with as remote of a possibility as it may seem, it is possible that you might produce sentences and books in this manner.[9]

If that seems wild and irresponsible, that's because it is. It's also why these evolutionists are

32

constantly seeking to increase the commonly accepted age of the universe. When you are dealing with the kind of astronomical odds that are required to accomplish particles-to-people evolution, you simply must have absurdly long amounts of time at your disposal, or an already absurd proposition becomes completely impossible. But the dirty little secret is that even with billions of years, it's still impossible. Why?

The crux of their entire theory that life can arise without a supernatural agency rests on the premise that information can be produced with no intelligence...just pure chance.

But that hope is obliterated when you consider one simple question: those words C-A-T or H-O-M-E that were spelled out by chance are words to whom? Only to those of us who speak English. In other words, you have to know the language for those letters to make any sense. The order of letters is meaningless unless there's a language or translation system already in place and established.[10]

And the same thing is true with DNA. Even if we were to concede the mathematically inconceivable notion that molecules ordered themselves perfectly by chance, life still isn't possible unless the machinery that makes those molecules function properly is already established and capable of reading the code. DNA without the language interpretation system is worthless. And now, are you ready for this? Guess what directs the language system to work right? DNA!

In other words, one couldn't have evolved into the other – both had to be there functioning at the same time for it to work. Which brings us to Problem 3.

Problem Three: "Rage Against the Machines"

I mentioned airplanes earlier. Have you paused to recognize that the various parts of a plane don't fly on their own? A wing won't fly by itself. The engine won't. Even the little nuts and bolts won't. The object only flies properly when it is completely constructed, down to the final screw. That's exactly the way it is with organisms. They can't and won't function properly unless the whole machine is constructed and operating together.

Consider the amazing human cell. Scientists once believed that the human cell was a simple entity, and that the various tasks it accomplished, like detecting light and turning it into electrical impulses, were simple processes. As it turns out, the exact opposite is true. A cell is a highly complicated structure, with all kinds of specialized operations that require multiple compounds being in just the right place at just the right time in just the right amount for the cell to function properly.[11]

In other words, just like the jet must have all those random parts in place to fly, a cell must have all its parts in place just to do the simple task of turning light into electrical impulses. And the same principle is true for all the other functions of the cells. Think of it this way: the nucleus of the cell – it's brain – could not have evolved from the cell membrane because the cell membrane needs the nucleus to function. But the membrane couldn't have evolved from the nucleus because the nucleus needs the membrane to function.

Each part or "biochemical machine" must be there at the same time, functioning in order for it to work. This reality is what led Dr. Michael Behe to state, "The simplicity that was once expected to be the foundation of life has proven to be a phantom; instead, systems of horrendous, irreducible complexity inhabit the cell."[12]

The scientists at the group *Answers in Genesis* further explain this principle using the example of a mosquito. When you swat a mosquito and smash it, all the information of that mosquito is still there – all the chemicals it had when it was alive are still present. Yet we know that the squashed "mosquito soup," as they call it, is not going to reassemble to life. How do we know that? Because we seriously disorganized the machinery by smashing it.[13]

See, even with all the chemicals there, you still must have the machinery in existence and operational, or life isn't possible from that mosquito soup. The same is true of the evolutionists' so-called primordial soup. Without the biochemical machinery already existing, evolution from chemicals is not just unlikely, it's impossible.

So what does all this mean? It means that the information that is in all life simply cannot arise by chance. Logic demands an intelligent agent with more information to make and create something with less information. All of our scientific and human experience indicates that is true. This is what I meant in the last chapter when I said that while science can't prove God, it does bear witness to His existence.

Dr. Werner Gitt agreed, stating,

"There is no known natural law through which matter can give rise to information, neither is any physical process or material phenomenon known that can do this...A code system is always the result of a mental process...All experiences indicate that a thinking being voluntarily exercising his own free will, cognition, and creativity, is required."[14]

The information in our human encyclopedia, or even the information in the amoeba encyclopedia, had to come from an intelligence vastly superior to us. Even leading evolutionists like Richard Dawkins accept this, which is why when their beliefs are challenged, they will suggest that perhaps life on earth was seeded by an alien race.[15] The Search for Extra-Terrestrial Intelligence, or SETI project was largely based on such a premise.[16]

To these evolutionists, that is a more acceptable conclusion than accepting the existence of God. But why? Dr. Behe answers that question for us:

"The...most powerful reason for science's reluctance to embrace a theory of intelligent design is also based on philosophical considerations. Many people, including many important and well-respected scientists, just don't want there to be anything beyond nature...In other words, they bring an *a priori* philosophical commitment (meaning a preconceived assumption) to their science that restricts what kinds of explanations they will accept about the physical world. Sometimes this leads to rather odd behavior."[17]

Certainly, believing that ET is more likely the source of life than God is "odd behavior." Here's the truth that many rational minds have acknowledged: if there is a God who created us, that same God owns us, and we are accountable to Him.[18]

It is *that* reality that drives the evolutionary mind to rebel against God and not accept the simplest conclusion before us. Not science.

3

"YOU CHOOSE FAITH OVER SCIENCE"

The Challenge

"Creationism, intelligent design, and other claims of supernatural intervention in the origin of life or of species are not science because they are not testable by the methods of science. These claims subordinate observed data to statements based on authority, revelation, or religious belief.

Documentation offered in support of these claims is typically limited to the special publications of their advocates. These publications do not offer hypotheses subject to change in light of new data, new interpretations, or demonstration of error. This contrasts with science, where any hypothesis or theory always remains subject to the possibility of rejection or modification in the light of new knowledge."[1]

- National Academy of Sciences

Hijacking Science

I remember flipping through the channels on rainy Saturday mornings when I was in junior high school and stopping every so often to watch the quirky antics of a program called *Bill Nye the Science Guy*. Bill was funny, entertaining...and as it turns out, pretty much convinced that I'm a child abuser. No, not in the physical sense, but rather I am battering my girls psychologically and intellectually.

In a video presentation posted to the online educational forum called Big Think, Nye begged Bible believing parents like my wife and I that even if we choose to live in a, "world that's completely inconsistent with everything we observe in the universe," to not expose our kids to that "God created the world" stuff. After all, he predicts, "In another couple centuries that worldview (Biblical Christianity), I'm sure...just won't exist."

And why won't it, you ask? Because according to Nye, "There's no evidence for it."[2] It's just silly faith.

The truth is that Nye is not even close to being alone. He is merely articulating the modern caricature that is well known: that you can either believe what the Bible says, or you can believe what science says. But for as widespread as what this claim has become and is becoming, it is predicated upon abject foolishness. In fact, such a claim itself hinges entirely on an unfair manipulation of the true nature and definition of science.

What is science? That's a question that could certainly be answered in a number of ways. But a generally accepted definition of the term would be this: the systematic study of the structure and behavior of the physical and natural world.

As a study, then, science will yield basic data. The study is full of theories, hypotheses, ideas that are tested, re-tested, examined, re-examined, observed, re-observed, proved or disproved as we collect more data. The results of those data collections are then interpreted by scientists to explain or undo certain concepts or models in our pursuit of knowledge and understanding.

To be more precise, it may be easier to understand what science is and what it is not by using an example. Suppose a discovery was made high in the mountains of Ararat, around modern day Turkey. Let's say that a group of mountain climbers and explorers found or uncovered a large, rectangular barge-like structure that appeared to be very old. Scientists, known as archaeologists, would then study its components, test the materials that make up the structure, and come to the conclusion, we'll suppose, that it is petrified wood.

Christians would immediately pounce on this find and announce the discovery of Noah's Ark. They would proclaim that science had vindicated the Biblical account of a global flood. Meanwhile, secular, anti-

Christian scientists who don't believe in a global flood would reject this conclusion, and would find some other explanation for the large, wooden structure.

Both groups of scientists would claim science was on their side. But both would be wrong. That's not to say that one of their conclusions might not be right. But claiming that science had proven their position wouldn't be right. Science is the process, the discovery and testing. It's the "study." Science would have revealed that large, wooden structure. From that point, differing people would work that scientific find into a narrative they had already accepted based on their own assumptions of the great philosophical questions. But notice that their narratives are based off of their worldview and preconceived philosophy...not science.

It's the same principle we can witness with fossil finds. After unearthing a previously undiscovered species in the rock strata, anti-Christian scientists might claim that given certain similarities it shares with a couple other species, they have discovered a transitional, missing link in the evolutionary chain. They claim science proves it. But science hasn't proven that at all. Science has revealed a fossil and various facts about its composition. The missing link explanation is part of a pre-accepted narrative those scientists adhere to and advocate.

Christian scientists would not ignore that discovery or pretend it doesn't exist. They wouldn't reject the "science," but they would probably reject the anti-Christian interpretation. The Bible-believing scientists would claim that perhaps the species is the discovery of one of God's unique creations that had been wiped out by the global flood, and that its similar bone structures to other creatures simply indicates that it had been designed to walk, eat or function in comparable ways.

See how this works? Science reveals the data. We interpret that data based largely on our assumptions. Historically, there is a tendency of both sides to attempt to hijack the term science in this way. Years ago, the church controlled the power structures of the scientific community, and anybody who espoused a different interpretation of science than the church was excommunicated, punished and ostracized.

Today, the exact same thing happens, except the other way around. Secular, anti-Christian scientists now control the scientific establishment (from academia to scholarly journals) and they ostracize anyone who has an alternative theory or explanation of scientific data than they do.

The truth is that there isn't much – if any – disagreement amongst Christian and anti-Christian scientists on 90% of scientific study and inquiry. Operational science as it's called – experiments, tests, data collection, observation – is conducted the same way by both groups. It's just as respected, just as valued, just as appreciated by both sides. The differences come when we start talking about what is called origin science.

Operational science involves empirical testing and experiments, like studying the spread of disease or the effects of zero-gravitation. Origin science, however, involves theoretical explanations of phenomena that can't be directly observed, like how the solar system originated, or how the Grand Canyon formed.

But don't overlook the critical point that when it comes to this origin science, since it is theoretical in nature and can't be directly observed, it isn't one side that is built on the back of faith and assumption...it's BOTH sides that are ultimately based on faith and assumption.

Famous evolutionist Harold Urey acknowledged as much when he admitted,

> "All of us who study the origin of life find that the more we look into it, the more we feel that it is too complex to have evolved anywhere. We all believe as an article of faith that life evolved from dead matter on this planet."[3]

Notice that key admission: those who believe that something came from nothing, without the involvement of a Supernatural Being, do so on the ultimate basis of faith.

Physicist Robert Jastrow concurred, stating,

> "Either life was created by the will of a

(supreme) being; or it evolved on our planet spontaneously. The first theory is a statement of faith in the power of a Supreme Being not subject to the laws of science. The second theory is also an act of faith. The act of faith consists in assuming that the scientific view is correct, without having concrete evidence to support that belief."[4]

Now, these quotes don't mean that the faith or assumptions held by the anti-Christian scientists are wrong. They simply mean that they are faith and assumptions. I am not suggesting that Jastrow or Urey were any less convinced that their view was correct. I am simply suggesting that they were intellectually honest enough to admit they were ultimately in the same boat as those who believe in a Designer: lacking observable data to prove their assumption.

In other words, the folks who believe in special creation by God because "the Bible tells them so" are no more guilty of relying on faith than the folks who believe in some cosmic naturalism by random processes because "Darwin or Spencer told them so." Both sides use real science and real data to explain and defend their theories and justify their faith.

But acknowledging that is more than some of the modern day neo-Darwinists can stomach. Take Paul Zachary Myers (better known as PZ Myers), a rather foul mouthed molecules-to-man evangelist who teaches as an associate professor of biology at the University of Minnesota Morris. This man, who describes himself as a "godless liberal biologist," had this to say about me and anyone else who doesn't accept his assumptions:

> "Neither macro nor micro evolution are speculative. Neither one is lacking in evidence. Heck was merely flaunting the tedious ignorance of creationists, which is no longer ever surprising. He was also making a dishonest pretense to knowledge, which is also not surprising, and is one reason to never, ever trust anyone who claims to be a creationist — it's a synonym for lying, stupid fraud."[5]

What Myers lacks in intellectual honesty, he attempts to veil with arrogance and a serial overuse of caustic pejoratives. Sadly, too many good Christians are intimidated by these tactics, and they cower beneath the unrelenting drumbeat from pop culture and the media that popularizes this common refrain that it is somehow "anti-science" to believe in the Bible. Let's consider some of their claims.

Claim One: Written by Idiots

Here's a portion of an email I received that embraces one of the more common lines of attack:

> "The Bible was written by uneducated authors some 2000 years ago. All of the writers were uninformed and certainly didn't comprehend the intricacies of 21st century science, so 21st century people shouldn't trust

their conclusions. Piece of advice, Heck: if the only book you read was written by idiots, time to buy a newer edition."

Lovely, isn't it? Now, there are three important things to note here:

First, it is ironic that the same standard my emailing friend uses to measure the intellect of the Biblical authors is apparently not applied to Charles Darwin – a man who had no knowledge of the intricate inner-workings of the cell at the time he authored his so-called masterpiece, *The Origin of Species*. For some reason, a man like Darwin, who later postulated in his work *The Descent of Man* some very backwards, ignorant, and racially offensive ideas is revered as a genius by those who would call the Biblical authors idiots or unreliable buffoons. That's some pretty sweet methodology.

Second, this email commits a fairly egregious logical fallacy, popularly called the "genetic fallacy." It is characterized by rejecting an idea because of its source. In other words, rather than testing the idea and letting it stand or fall on its merit, you reject it because of whoever suggested it. Now, that doesn't mean that we should ignore the source or the authors of a work. Looking at and examining the authors might be a helpful thing to do in explaining how or why they came to their conclusions. But it is totally irrelevant in assessing whether what they are saying is accurate.

Third (and this is the most important), according

to Scripture, these human authors weren't actually the authors of the Bible at all. 2 Timothy 3:16 famously declares that "All Scripture is God-breathed,"[6] meaning the God of the universe – who created the laws of science – is the author of the text, utilizing human pens to record His words. If one accepts Scripture, the human error is eliminated from the equation entirely.

Claim Two: The Bible is a Religious Text, Not a Science Text

Another common argument goes that even if you want to accept the Bible, you should use it for its purpose. And its purpose, they say, was to teach morality or even salvation, not to teach science. Fair enough. But saying the Bible was not intended to be a science book is a far cry from saying the Bible is unscientific or scientifically inaccurate. No one would confuse *The Scarlet Letter* with a history text book, but that doesn't mean its historical references or allusions are incorrect. The Biblical text is unquestionably a revelation of God's unrelenting redemptive plan for His creation. But that doesn't mean that when the Bible speaks of scientific things, the Bible is wrong.

In fact, when it comes to its science, the Bible has a better track record than...well...science. It was Galileo who proved that we were surrounded by a universe of innumerable stars rather than the few thousand that the scientific community once taught. Yet the unscientific Bible was proclaiming thousands of years earlier in Jeremiah 33:22, "*Countless as the stars* of the sky and as measureless as the sand on the seashore."

It wasn't until the 20th century that deep sea technology revealed to us that some of the largest mountain ranges in the world were actually at the bottom of the oceans. But the famous account of Jonah and the Great Fish, found in that unscientific Bible, actually told us in Jonah 2:5-6, "The engulfing waters threatened me, the deep surrounded me; seaweed wrapped around my head. To the *roots of the mountains* I sank down."

Science now understands that we live in a universe that, as unbelievable as it seems given its already gargantuan size, is spreading out. But the old prophet Isaiah, writing in that unscientific Bible, was telling us the same thing thousands of years ago when he testified in chapter 40, verse 22 that God, "...*stretches out* the heavens like a canopy."

And what about the shape and position of the earth in space? The scientific community not only held for generations that the earth was flat, but it also entertained the most peculiar theories of how the earth was held up in the universe. It wasn't until the days of the explorers that we realized the earth was spherical, and it wasn't until much later that science confirmed that the earth was "suspended over nothing" in space. Yet, once again, the unscientific Bible had the answer to both these questions long ago. Isaiah wrote in that same passage that God, "sits enthroned above the circle (or sphere) of the earth," and in Job 26:7 we read that, "He suspends the earth over nothing."

We're still not done. Even though the water
cycle seems pretty simple to us now, it was a scientific
mystery for centuries. Where did rain come from?
How did the oceans maintain their size? Many credit a
16th century scientist with the discovery of the
hydrologic cycle – how water evaporates from lakes
and oceans, condenses above the earth and returns to
the land in the form of precipitation. Others say the
cycle wasn't clearly understood or defined until as late
as the 20th century. But the truth is that one of the
oldest manuscripts in the unscientific Bible, the Book of
Job (36:27), explained it all perfectly long before
modern science: "He draws up the drops of water,
which distill as rain to the streams." Or if Job wasn't
good enough, how about Amos 5:8 that explains how
God, "…calls for the waters of the sea and pours them
out over the face of the land."

Given these startling realities, which only begin
to uncover the profound scientific accuracy of the Bible,
it certainly is difficult to allege the text is unscientific.
And if that doesn't persuade you, consider this: outside
of supernatural events that transpire by God's
intentional acts which transcend our physical laws (the
sun standing still in Joshua, the parting of the Red Sea
in Exodus), secular scientists cannot point to a singular
scientific claim in the Bible that is inaccurate.

**Claim Three: "The Bible Tells Me So" Is
Unsophisticated**

If there is one area where anti-Christian skeptics
have been successful, it is at convincing Bible believing

Christians that there is something unsophisticated about leaning on the Bible as the starting point of our worldview. It's a peculiar phenomenon that usually goes like this:

> **Skeptic**: "Why do you think abortion is wrong?"
> **Christian**: "Well, because the Bible teaches that…"
> **Skeptic**: "Ah, ah, well, I and many others don't accept the Bible, so you have to argue using something else."

And we actually feel it necessary to accept that logic. We feel obligated to assume worldly assumptions and try to argue from a starting point we don't accept. It should come as no surprise that such an approach doesn't work out well for us. Why would it?! Notice that secularists would never do this. Try approaching that conversation the exact opposite way:

> **Christian**: "Why don't you believe in God?"
> **Skeptic**: "Well, I think Darwin's explanation of the origin…"
> **Christian**: "Ah, ah, well, I and many others don't accept Darwin, so you start with the Bible which I do accept and use it to explain why you don't believe in God."

They would never agree to abandoning their own starting point and assumptions. So why do we? This is exactly what happens on secular college campuses around America today. We typically warn of Christian kids going to face these ungodly professors who spend each day ranting and raving about how foolish the Bible is and why it shouldn't be believed. But the truth is that really doesn't happen...or at least not regularly. No, what really happens is that the Bible is just ignored.

The professors begin their explanations from worldly assumptions and just expect their students to do the same. The starting point is pre-determined, and if you have a different starting point, you better figure out how to assume another one pretty fast or you're lost. All conclusions that are accepted in that course, then, naturally prove the validity of the original worldly starting point, making it appear to impressionable young people that the evidence validates the original godless assumptions. It's a vicious circular reasoning that traps far more minds than we want to admit.

The truth is that all our thinking – in science, the arts, philosophy – will start from basic assumptions. Saying my assumptions are based on what the Bible tells me is no more anti-intellectual than saying my assumptions are based on what some man or group of men have told me.

There is simply no getting around the fact that we will all accept some faith, some presuppositions, in order to build our lives and our worldviews. The debate we should be having then, is simply this: is the wisdom of man's words or the wisdom of the Bible's words the more reliable foundation?

4

"The Bible's Not Reliable"

The Challenge

You've got a book of myths, for which no historical proof actually exists! If you had any proof, you wouldn't need faith, and preachers wouldn't have to try to convince people that faith (the bypassing of one's brain) is a virtue, and call it what it really is, downright stupidity. The Bible is full of BS stories, like making man from the dirt or clay or whatever, 'miracles', virgin births and all kinds of other things, which seemed to cease occurring at exactly the same time that humanity began to learn methods for investigating and debunking such claims (the scientific method).

Just because some of these towns exist, or some of the wars existed, does not give any support at all to the supernatural events which are said to have occurred in them.

The Christian myth is a rip-off of other contemporary beliefs, and was written in such a way to convince people at *the time that it must have been true, based on their existing beliefs. We see evidence for this tactic in the traditions that go with Christmas, such as tree decorations and their choice of date. The rest of it was just made up. It was made up by a bunch of Stone-Age men, many of them extremely violent and brutal, with no understanding of the world around them. It has absolutely no more weight than any other ancient book of fairy tales.[1]* – AtheistPropaganda.com

The Big Questions

In chapter one, we established the philosophical truth of the existence of some *Beyond*, and deduced on the basis of complexity logic, that this *Beyond* must be indeed personal – a being or entity that is complex, or at least as complex as we are.

We also noted how restless we are as humans – constantly wondering about who we are, how we got here, and where we're going...the big questions. Just turn on your TV or listen to your radio and you realize how imbedded these questions are into our human psyche. The entire history of mankind has revealed an obsession with attempting to explain and satisfy this grand curiosity.

We really want answers. But it doesn't take too long to realize that on our own, we can never figure them out. This is one of those high-minded philosophical truths: starting with the finite (which man unquestionably is), you can never get to the infinite. If what we have around us, what we can know, understand and observe, is confined inside that little plastic kickball we referred to earlier, we will never be able to put parameters around, grasp or comprehend all that's going on outside of that ball.

So where does that leave us and exactly what does it mean? It means that we are in need of some answers and guidance – some communication – from that *Person Beyond* if we're ever going to make sense out of all this...or at least make some sense out of it. Here's what the great thinker Socrates said on his deathbed:

> "All the wisdom of this world is but a tiny raft upon which we must set sail when we leave this earth. If only there was a firmer foundation upon which to sail, perhaps some divine word."[2]

Don't overlook what Socrates just did for us. He answered the question we ended the last chapter asking: are the Bible's words or man's words more reliable? If the Bible is what it claims to be (the revelation of God to man), then there is simply no question that it provides a more stable guide and secure foundation point for our thinking. Just ask Socrates, popularly considered the greatest of all human thinkers. So then, are the Bible's claims to be a revelation from God actually true?

Proof One: The 3 D's

First, it's vital that we note the Bible makes the outrageous and audacious claim hundreds of times to be the Word of God Himself. Don't understate that claim. This isn't wishy-washy stuff, hinting that it might be divine in nature, but at the same time providing itself a way out or some escape clause. The Bible never claims to be a simple guide for moral behavior or insights into religious character, or a compilation of supreme wisdom and noble thoughts. It says without equivocation it is the Word of God.

There's no wiggle room here for anyone who seeks to render a judgment on the Biblical text: it's either a Deceptive Book, a Deranged Book, or a Divine Book.[3] Now, that is certainly noteworthy because it's what we should expect from any communication that came from a *God Beyond*. If He did give us something, if He gave us *anything*, we'd expect it to be overtly and daringly authoritative.

And not just authoritative, but unique. Very unique. Certainly the Bible could be characterized no other way. Look at the other religious texts in the world and you see how very different the Bible is from all of them. That doesn't mean there aren't any similarities, of course. You see the moral ethic of "doing unto others as you would have them do unto you" reflected in multiple religious traditions. But the crux of the Bible's message, meaning the way it confronts the serious moral failings of mankind (and the consequences brought on by those failings), is remarkably unique.

Every other grand religious text teaches to overcome those moral failings by living better, which is usually defined as becoming enlightened, transcending the earthly and the material realm, walking a religious pathway, meditating, or envisioning goodness. But not the Bible. In fact, the Bible bluntly tells us that the solution is totally out of our hands. It says do all those wonderful things and if compared to God, they are filthy rags. It tells us to do good deeds, but if that's all we've got, we'll still go to Hell because God demands perfection.

See what I mean? The Bible is totally unique. Every other religious text shows man reaching up to God as the solution, saying "do these things," "act this way," "complete these practices" to make it all okay. But the Bible contradicts that philosophy, saying in essence, "reach up to God all you want and you'll never make it." I don't mean to suggest that the Bible's emphasis on man's depravity is cause for despair, of course – just that it offers a completely unique solution to our desperate state.[4] Instead of man reaching up to his God, the Bible is the only text that shows God reaching down to man to rectify his hopeless situation. It's what we would expect from a Divine Text, isn't it? Total uniqueness.

But of course, just pointing out the uniqueness of the Bible, or that it claims to be the Word of God, doesn't make it so. It would be the height of circular reasoning to say things like:

> **Skeptic**: "But how do you know that Scripture is from God?"
> **Christian**: "Well, it's in the Bible."
> **Skeptic**: "But do you know the Bible is true?"

Christian: "Well, 2 Timothy 3:16 says the
Bible is from God, and God wouldn't lie."[5]

If you really want to tick off a skeptic...argue that
way. But even though the uniqueness of Scripture and
its claim to be the inspired of Word of God are not
proof in themselves, they are quite relevant and
significant for us to note. The Bible's human authors
were obviously all under the impression they were
writing with the inspiration and authority of God. But
how can we judge if their impressions were accurate?
Well first, if they were divinely inspired, we should see
some unworldly and inexplicable consistency in their
words, as well as a profound authenticity in the
preservation of their work.

Proof Two: Consistency and Authenticity

Remember that the Bible is a compilation of 66
books. These 66 books were written by over 40
different authors (the vast majority of whom didn't
know each other), written on three different continents,
in three different languages, over a span of almost 2,000
years. Imagine attempting something so grand even
today in our era of amazing connectivity and
communication. Such an undertaking would
unquestionably result in numerous inconsistencies,
errors and contradictions, no matter how hard we tried.
Now imagine attempting something like this in ancient
times. There is simply no logical or credible way you
can assume human beings alone were capable of
producing such an amazingly complex volume of
books with such a clarified and consistent message.

Something else had to be involved.

To be fair, there are still many leading skeptics who argue that there are plenty of inconsistencies to be found in the Biblical text. Yet those claims rely on increasingly flimsy evidence and some easily dismissed translation flaws. In fact, in the past 6 decades alone, the most credible and concerning accusations against the Bible's self-consistency have evaporated in light of research and discovery. In other words, the more reliable our investigation and examination of the Scriptures become, the less questions we have about its accuracy. That is simply stunning.

Remember, this is no simple text. It tells the story of the creation of the universe, the origin of life, the rise and fall of several ancient civilizations, the historical biography of the life of Jesus, details of the ancient world and so much more. Yet even the most ardent skeptics cannot point to a single, credible inconsistency in the Biblical message. To any student of literature – particularly ancient literature – that is astounding. Actually, it's more than astounding. It is miraculous.

But that's not all. The surviving copies of Biblical manuscripts make it the single most authenticated text in all of ancient literature…and it's not even close. For historians, the two primary tests for authenticity involve the age of the surviving copies and the number of surviving copies. In terms of the first test, the smaller the length of time that exists between the oldest copy we have and the time of the writing of the original, the better. And as far as the second test, the more consistent copies of the ancient text that have been preserved, the better.

On both of those counts, the Bible stands alone at the top.[6] What does this mean? If a skeptic wants to argue that the Bible can't be trusted because it lacks authenticity to the original, consistency demands that they MUST dismiss all other works of antiquity – Josephus, Tacitus, Plutarch – as unreliable and inauthentic. If a scholar attempts to question Biblical claims on authenticity grounds, he is compelled to hold other works to the same standard, which means questioning whether Plato really existed or whether Alexander the Great really conquered. Because those histories – as accurate as we believe them to be – are far less substantiated and authenticated than Scripture.

Proof Three: Prophetic Insight

Another corroborating fact in proving the reliability of the Scriptural claim to be divinely inspired is its remarkably accurate prophetic history. There are, scattered throughout the pages of Scripture, hundreds of predictions and prophecies of people and events yet to come. Some of those are general and generic, while others are precise and detailed. In a spine-tingling statement on the authority of the Bible, with the notable exception of the events surrounding the second coming of Christ, there isn't a single one of those events predicted by Scripture that failed to occur. Not one.

One of the most profound examples took place

in the 2nd chapter of Daniel, where the author predicts three successive world empires, and their subsequent collapses. Daniel was written hundreds and hundreds of years before some of those civilizations even existed. Yet now, with those events 2000 years in our rear view mirror, we can see that they occurred exactly as the Bible predicted. Being a skeptic is fine, but common sense requires the acknowledgement that there's something going on there beyond guessing and dumb luck.

And besides the prophecies, archaeology has been useful in confirming Scriptural locations and accounts that skeptics once mocked as myth. For instance, the recent excavation of Jericho found that the city walls had collapsed in a way consistent with Joshua's account. And the unearthing of ancient trade documents has revealed routes that included the five "cities of the plain" that are referenced in Genesis 14:2 - cities that secularists once dismissed as non-existent.[7]

Proof Four: A Solid Foundation

Yet despite all these corroborating facts, the truth is that the previous "proofs" I've been giving aren't really proofs. That word implies that there can be no questioning any of them, and that isn't true. The secularist is entitled to object to each of them. As irresponsible or silly as it might be, they can claim chance or luck in the Bible's stunningly accurate predictive prophecy. They can claim that the archaeological finds vindicating and validating the Biblical historical record are being misidentified or misinterpreted. They can claim the reason the Bible seems so consistent is because Christians have manipulated and corrected it through the years.

No, these proofs aren't really proofs. They are evidence – evidence that the Bible is true. But in order to really know for certain that the Bible is reliable, there needs to be something more concrete and irrefutable. Piggybacking on a discussion we had earlier in the book, how about this: if the Bible wasn't true, we could know *nothing*.[8]

Seems melodramatic, doesn't it? I even used italics to make you read it dramatically. But think about it the way Dr. Jason Lisle explains it in his essay, "How Do We Know the Bible is True?" In each of the evidences we examined, we lean on certain standards to prove our positions correct. We use the standard of science or the standards of logic or the standards of mathematics in making our case. And the secularist does the same thing to state his position, relying on certain standards in hopes of justifying his claims.

But here's the shocker: apart from the Bible, there are (and can ultimately be) no standards at all. Scripture tells us in multiple places that God is a fixed point...constant and consistent. It tells us that His laws of nature will remain unchanged. It tells us that His mind is the standard for all knowledge. If the Bible wasn't right about that and could not be trusted, we would have no guarantee that these standards we use would be unchanging, and thus reliable. We would have no ability to reason, debate, discuss or argue. Yet that is what we are doing.

Only a Biblical worldview can make sense of the universal, no-exceptions, unchanging nature of the laws of logic. Because the God who is beyond those laws has assured us in His revelation, the Bible, that they will remain consistent and steadfast for us to lean on, we can have faith enough to use them reliably. The secularist has no such confidence. Even if he proclaims to believe in "unchanging natural laws," he can have no assurance that those natural laws will never change. Therefore, he is reduced to using those laws and standards only in...are you ready for this ironic twist..."blind faith."[9]

It's honestly one of the funniest – but also saddest – realities to observe: men who deny the existence of God and the truth of the Bible, going out and unintentionally relying on the existence of God and the promises of the Bible to make their case against them.

How is that possible? Romans 1:18-21 tells us that God has revealed Himself to all men. He hardwired us with the awareness that He is. Men may suppress that truth in unrighteousness, but oblivious to their own inconsistency, they still rely on it.

The worldview expressed in the Bible is the only one that can make sense of the standards and laws necessary to obtain knowledge and develop reason. Unless we presuppose the truth of the Bible, we couldn't prove or conclude anything at all. That, my friends, makes the Bible not just reliable. It makes it irreplaceable.

Exactly what you would expect if it were Divine.

5

"THE RESURRECTION IS A MYTH"

The Challenge

During the 19 years I preached the Gospel, the resurrection of Jesus was the keystone of my ministry...But now I no longer believe it. Many bible scholars and ministers--including one third of the clergy in the Church of England--reject the idea that Jesus bodily came back to life. So do 30% of born-again American Christians!

Why? When the Gospel of John portrays the post-mortem Jesus on a fishing trip with his buddies and the writer of Matthew shows him giving his team a mountain-top pep talk two days after he died, how can there be any doubt that the original believers were convinced he had bodily risen from the grave?

There have been many reasons for doubting the claim,

BEL**i**EVE

*but the consensus among critical scholars today appears to be
that the story is a "legend." During the 60-70 years it took
for the Gospels to be composed, the original story went
through a growth period that began with the unadorned idea
that Jesus, like Grandma, had "died and gone to heaven" and
ended with a fantastic narrative produced by a later
generation of believers that included earthquakes, angels, an
eclipse, a resuscitated corpse, and a spectacular bodily
ascension into the clouds.*

*The earliest Christians believed in the "spiritual"
resurrection of Jesus. The story evolved over time into a
"bodily" resurrection.*[1]   *– Dan Barker*

The Greatest Moment

As a history teacher, one of the most common
questions I get from students and others is what I think
is the single greatest moment in human history. It
doesn't even take me to the end of their question to
give them the answer: the physical resurrection of Jesus
of Nazareth from the grave.

I have to admit that I find it very odd that the
anti-Christian secularists spend as much time as they
do arguing philosophically about the existence of a
Divine Being, or quarreling about scientific
interpretations in their war against Christianity. The
reason I'm confused by that is because this singular
issue is their silver bullet. If they truly want to destroy
Christianity – if that is the objective – then simply
undermine the truth of the resurrection, and the rest of
the faith becomes meaningless.

The alleged triumph of Jesus over death is the linchpin upon which everything in Christianity hinges. Even the Apostle Paul admitted that, writing to the Corinthians, "If Christ has not been raised, your faith is futile; you are still in your sins."[2] See what I mean? This question of the resurrection of Christ is the whole ballgame when it comes to the Christian faith. If Jesus didn't resurrect from the dead, nothing else matters for believers. So, can we be confident that it really occurred?

The Givens

To keep with my original goal of writing a book that is succinct and readable rather than an epic text that, while loaded with information, sits unmoved on the shelves of busy people, let's establish what we are not going to be arguing here. Given the abundance of evidence that has been provided to prove and validate them, here are four facts that I am assuming as accepted truth for the purposes of this discussion.

First, Jesus was a real person who actually walked the earth. It was really an interesting phenomenon while it lasted. Though we had better records and more reliable evidence for the existence of Jesus of Nazareth than say, Plato, there would occasionally be scholars who would bizarrely attempt to argue that Jesus wasn't a real person; that he was just a character from a book. None of these same scholars would question the existence of Plato, of course, or even of other religious leaders like Mohammed. But they seemed to delight in indulging this ridiculous intellectual fantasy where they called into question the physical existence of Jesus. It's safe to say that today, with all the extra-biblical confirmations of His life from sources like Josephus and Tacitus, there is no serious or credible question about whether Jesus really existed. It's a silly argument made by silly minds.

Second, there is no real debate whether Jesus of Nazareth performed miraculous signs and wonders that amazed the people of His day. Even those testifying against Jesus' claims – hostile witnesses to his life, mission and teaching – accuse Jesus in ancient writings of performing black magic, and doing things by the power of the devil. In other words, they implicitly acknowledge that Jesus was performing those miraculous signs, while merely calling into question the source of His power.

Third, there is no credible reason to doubt that Jesus died a physical death on a cross during a public crucifixion. Simple study of the brutality of Roman executions – particularly crucifixions – should answer any question as to whether His executioners knew how to finish the job. But beyond that, eyewitness testimony of the merciless beating He received, the reported symptoms He experienced that were consistent with life-threatening conditions like hypovolemic shock, and the spear through His side that ruptured membranes of internal organs leave no doubt. Not to mention the fact that the Roman soldiers presiding over His execution knew they would meet the same fate if somehow their victim survived. When

Jesus came down from the cross, He was physically dead.

As an intellectual exercise, consider the hypothetical situation where Jesus wasn't really dead – but had just slipped out of consciousness due to blood loss. As explained by numerous Christian apologists, this ridiculous theory would demand that Jesus' mangled, abused, bleeding and tormented body on the doorstep of death was laid in a cold, dank tomb with no medical attention, food or water. Then, in three days woke up, felt and looked great, single handedly pushed the giant boulder out of the way and started running through the hills proclaiming to be the exalted, resurrected Messiah. Nonsense. Jesus was assuredly dead.

Fourth, there is simply no question that the tomb of Jesus was empty on that third day. Remember that this tomb was well known to Christians and Jews alike. If it weren't empty – if Jesus' body was still laying cold inside – there is no logical explanation for how a movement based on the resurrection could have started right there. Does anyone seriously doubt that had the Jewish authorities who had called for Jesus' crucifixion, or the Romans who had carried it out, had any access to the dead body of Jesus, they would have put it on a cart and paraded it through the streets once the story began to circulate about a resurrection? As it's been said, this act would have single handedly strangled Christianity in its cradle.

And consider the guards' report that was

circulated in those days that the disciples of Jesus had come in the night and stole His body. As ridiculous a premise as it is (the same disciples who denied and abandoned Him suddenly became daring, courageous stealth commandos), the fact that the guards settled on this as their explanation is remarkably significant. Why? Because they are acknowledging the tomb is empty. Justin and Tertullian, ancient writers from the era immediately following the birth of the Christian church, both confirm this is exactly the story that the Jews of that day were spreading. They were trying to convince people what happened to the body, not telling people that the tomb still held the body of Christ. It's simply incontrovertible that the tomb of Jesus was vacant that third day.

But let's not get carried away and pretend that an empty tomb proves that there was a resurrection. Skeptics often accuse Christians of committing this logical fallacy by pointing out that, "The tomb could have been empty for a number of reasons other than a resurrection."

That's quite true. But Christians do not base their confidence in the resurrection simply on the reality of an empty tomb. They base it on the fact that there was a dead body laid in a tomb that later appeared to people alive and in the flesh. If that occurred – if the physical Jesus did, in fact, appear to people after his death – there can be no denying that the resurrection stands as the single greatest moment in human history. So how do we know it happened?

Evidence for the Resurrection: Pentecost

There are multiple accounts throughout the Gospel books of Matthew, Mark, Luke and John that depict Jesus appearing to people after his death. And remember in the last chapter we saw that according to ancient literature standards for accuracy, those books are four of the most authenticated and reliable texts we possess. But even more than the numerous examples of Jesus' appearances in those Gospels, is the testimony of Paul in his first letter to the Corinthians. After listing off a handful of individuals that the resurrected Jesus appeared to, he writes:

> "After that, he appeared to more than five hundred of the brothers and sisters at the same time, most of whom are still living, though some have fallen asleep."[3]

500 eyewitnesses is pretty compelling in the book of any fair minded person. But notice what Paul points out about many of those 500...they are still alive.

What that means is that if Paul was full of it – if he was embellishing or giving a false impression of the numerous witnesses to the resurrected Jesus – they could have spoken up and contradicted his account. In other words, the resurrection can't be a lie fabricated by just 11 of Jesus' friends. If it's a lie, it would have to be a plot orchestrated and maintained by hundreds of people. One of the most respected historians I have ever met, Dr. Edwin M. Yamauchi, comments on this fact:

"What gives a special authority to the list (of witnesses) as historical evidence is the reference to most of the 500 brethren being still alive. St. Paul says, in effect, 'If you do not believe me, you can ask them.' Such a statement in an admittedly genuine letter written within 30 years of the event is almost as strong evidence as one could hope to get for something that happened nearly 2000 years ago."[4]

But beyond just that, the most compelling argument here is what the sightings of a resurrected Jesus provokes: the birth of the Christian church. Don't overlook the fact that Christianity wasn't started in a distant land whose inhabitants had no working knowledge of the plot line. No, Christianity – a religion predicated upon a belief in the resurrection of Jesus – started in the very city where Jesus was killed and buried.

For some reason, thousands of people – many of whom didn't have anything to do with Jesus when He was alive – gathered together after his death to hear one of his apostles preach about how He had risen and why they should follow Him. What could possibly explain their interest in such an outlandish claim?

Maybe we get the answer as to what motivated their interest in the midst of Peter's message, when he proclaims, "God has raised this Jesus to life, and we are all witnesses of it."[5] *We* are *all* witnesses? What does that reveal? It reveals that many in the crowd were there because they saw the resurrected Christ. They had witnessed it.

As if that weren't enough, just a few sentences later, Peter repeats that same point, stating, "You killed the author of life, but God raised him from the dead. We are witnesses of this."[6] Do you know what this means? Perhaps we're not talking about hundreds of people who had seen the resurrected Christ. Perhaps we're talking thousands, given that thousands were present when Peter spoke of how they were all witnesses to the resurrection. And remember that thousands joined this upstart Christian church that very day.

Don't forget these were people who weren't following Jesus when He was alive. Why would they now, after He was dead? Why would they be "cut to the heart" as Scripture says? And further, keep in mind who we are talking about here.

Evidence for the Resurrection: Changing Course

If there was one group of people who exemplified and typified tradition, it was the Jewish people. In fact, it was their strict allegiance to their sacred traditions and customs – things like abstaining from work on the Sabbath and strict obedience to the Mosaic Law – that caused them to reject Christ in the first place.

Yet just five weeks after they saw Him put to

death (many having likely been vocal proponents of His execution), they are flocking to become His followers. And not just some. About 10,000. That's incredible. After all, while you might be able to explain away a few, a mass conversion of 10,000 people committing themselves to a belief in the same claims that caused them to reject Jesus in the first place, is spine-tingling evidence for something truly astonishing having occurred. Moreover, many of those who became followers were some of the biggest skeptics Jesus had during His ministry. Skeptics like James, Jesus' half-brother, who was embarrassed of Him. Skeptics like Saul, a guy who (until his conversion) went around killing followers of Jesus.

What caused that? What could generate that kind of buzz and provoke that kind of intense change of heart among so many people? Well maybe there's more than one answer, but one of them would certainly be the knowledge that a dead body had come back to life and been witnessed by hundreds, if not thousands of people.

Evidence for the Resurrection: Martyrs

And what about those who professed this resurrection claim in the very face of death? Certainly devoted individuals dying for a cause they believe in is nothing new or unique to our world. Countless men and women have done so since the dawn of recorded history. So it may not seem that persuasive at first glance to say that Christ's disciples died horrible deaths (as we know many of them did) because they refused to stop spreading the story of the resurrection.

Indeed, one need only think of the suicide hijackers of September 11, 2001 to see that even in our modern era, there are deluded individuals willing to go to their deaths for claims we know to be false. Their amazing conviction and commitment to those false beliefs obviously doesn't make them true. But there's something different going on here with Christ's disciples. In his epic work, *The Case for Christ*, author Lee Strobel put it best by explaining while men will die for their beliefs if they sincerely believe them to be true, they will not die for their beliefs if they know those beliefs are false.[7] That's the difference with the disciples of Jesus.

If you and I choose to die for our faith, we will do so because we have chosen to trust in the words and the testimony of Christ's resurrection that has been passed down through the ages. We trust others' words enough to die, though we can't know for sure if they told the truth. If we had reason to believe, or evidence to think the story wasn't true, I can at least tell you from my perspective that I would seriously rethink sacrificing my life, or even my time and money for such a cause. And certainly if we knew that our cause was a lie, we would never agree to die just to fool others into believing it. The disciples of Jesus were in that unique position of knowing.

If they stole the body away, if they manufactured the myth of Jesus' resurrection, if they knew their story wasn't true, then they knew they were dying horrible deaths for a lie. The fact that none of them ever recanted is really profound evidence for the truth of their claims.

What More Could He Have Done?

So where does that leave us? If you were approached by a person who began to argue with you, saying that George Washington was not the first president of the United States of America, you would quickly realize that, short of inventing a time machine, you could never prove your case beyond any doubt.

Sure, the historical record, including Washington's official portraits and hand-written correspondence, indeed everything we have, rely on and trust in historical documentation, would prove you correct. But if your Washington skeptic wanted to continue postulating the absurd theory that it was all an elaborate hoax set in motion by charlatans seeking power and profit and insisting that you were nothing but a dupe for believing it because, "After all, George might not have even existed," that would be his prerogative. All the rational explanations, historical testimony and corroborating evidence will fall on deaf ears. We must realize that such absurdity is what some will choose when it comes to the resurrection of Jesus.

Ask yourself, for this event happening in the time period in which it happened, what more could Jesus have done to 'prove' His resurrection to His contemporaries? Over the course of a month and a half, He appeared to a wide variety of people, in a wide variety of settings; He appeared to skeptics and even close-minded opponents; He allowed others to touch His body to test and see if it was real flesh; He ate with them, He spoke and responded to them, and He even cooked for them. What else could He have done? What more evidence could He have provided?

When it comes to the account of the resurrection of Jesus, what we can now say is that it is as authenticated an event in antiquity as we can point to. The skeptics' stories are weak, relying on speculation and circumstantial evidence at best. The weight of the historical record bears down heavily on the side of the resurrection.

So much so that Professor Thomas Arnold, author of the famous work *History of Rome* and chair of modern history at Oxford – a man who sets the gold standard for knowing how to determine historical facts – has affirmed,

> "I have been used for many years to study the histories of other times, and to examine and weigh the evidence of those who have written about them, and I know of no one fact in the history of mankind which is proved by better and fuller evidence of every sort, to the understanding of a fair inquirer, than the great sign which God hath given us that Christ died and rose from the dead."[8]

2,000 years later, the implications of the empty tomb and resurrected Christ still intimidate men into rebellion and denial. Can we really be surprised that if even after seeing or hearing about this miracle themselves, men and women of Jesus' day still rejected Him, that there are those two millennia later who choose the same? At least they have had time to come up with more excuses.

Nevertheless, we can now say this with confidence: One: Jesus of Nazareth was put to death on a cross and laid in a tomb. Two: That tomb of Jesus was empty three days later. Three: Hundreds, if not thousands of eyewitnesses saw the resurrected Jesus.

What you conclude and how you respond to those realities – whether they change the way you live or not – is up to you.

6

"GOD MUST BE A SADISTIC MONSTER"

The Challenge

"Is God willing to prevent evil, but not able? Then He is not omnipotent. Is he able, but not willing? Then He is malevolent. Is he both able, and willing? Then whence cometh evil? Is he neither able nor willing? Then why call Him God?"[1] – Epicurus

"If everything is designed, this leads one to conclude that all of the pain and suffering we see is not just the result of an indifferent universe, but instead the intentional product of a sadistic designer."[2] – Christopher Smotherman

Tough Accusations

This might seem surprising for me to say, but on

the surface, I don't think it's too tough to make the case that God must be some kind of sadist. After all, He has the power to prevent all suffering, so why doesn't He? And even if He allows some difficulties and hardships for us as a consequence of our poor decisions, why doesn't He at least prevent the suffering for innocent little children or infants who are completely guiltless and helpless? Just seeing toddlers who are victims of car accidents or infants in a children's hospital burn unit can quickly cause you to concoct the notion that any God who would allow that misery must be cruel beyond words.

If that seems unreasonable to say, make it personal. If you had the power to stop the sorrow, would you? The fact that God does have the power, but doesn't stop it sure seems like proof of His cruelty. And from a broader perspective, how could a loving God create a race of humans knowing that He would end up sending some of them to Hell? Wouldn't or shouldn't that deter an all-loving God from going ahead with the plan?

Let me pause here to say that in this and the remaining chapters, we are going to take on some real pointed and hard accusations against the character of God. Some of them may make you uncomfortable. They certainly make me feel that way. But these indictments are some of the most effective stumbling blocks that the enemy uses to create distance between us and our loving God. Therefore, we must understand them, and know how to deal with and respond to them.

I also want to add that for these next four chapters, I will lean heavily on some of the great research that Biblical scholar Glenn Miller has produced at the online Christian Think Tank (www.christianthinktank.com). While I am going to try to put a more layman's touch on these issues, for those who are interested into digging deep into these kinds of philosophical challenges, his Christian Think Tank is an excellent, blessed resource.

Who Do We Think We Are?

We need to begin with a basic understanding of the inherent logical flaws in what we are attempting to do when we morally accuse the Creator. What I mean is that when we position ourselves in such a way that we can deem God cruel or sadistic, we are presuming to be capable of judging the morality of God and His character on the basis of our own understanding. That's a real problem – whether you say you believe in God or not.

If we begin with the assumption that God does not exist, and we are merely trying to prove that the God of this mythical book called the Bible is not loving or moral, think about what we're doing. We begin with a creature – soulless, spiritless – who has, through billions of years of downright vicious struggle, surfaced at the top of all other beings. Through the evolutionary process of survival of the fittest, man has emerged from a savage history of proving superiority over other species by maiming them, killing them, devouring them, or totally annihilating them.

All of this is warranted and acceptable, of course, because it is the one law of nature: self-preservation. Whatever it takes to survive is justified in the evolutionary chain. With that as our background and identity, could we really with a straight face suggest that such a creature – one that has dominated and destroyed countless species on its way to the top – is even capable of articulating or making any moral judgments?

In the evolutionary, materialistic, no-God, no-soul mindset, all our decisions revolve around our own self-interest and self-preservation. So why would we ever think that our judgments on morality would come anywhere close to being objective and fair? It's simply illogical. Glenn Miller concludes,

> "To agree that a mudball with hair and teeth, red in tooth and fang," – that would be us – "can transcend this history to the point of making authoritative statements about morality and character, is well beyond my skeptical limits."[3]

Indeed. So then let's accept that God does exist. When we accuse Him of cruelty, what we're attempting is just as logically flawed. We somehow assume that God created a lesser being with a better heart, and a better sense of morality than Him. That's inconceivable. Remember, we discussed earlier the impossibility of the "effect" being greater than the "cause." Or, as Miller puts it, consider that another way of viewing this intellectual incongruity would be to suggest, "I have a greater intelligence than the absolute source of intelligence."[4] It just doesn't make sense.

Which brings us to an important but perhaps intimidating conclusion: as much as we may feel entitled to an explanation of why God does or doesn't do certain things, we are in no place to demand it. He is God, and we are not. We know of God what He has chosen to reveal to us. Maybe we will find answers to our questions in what He's revealed to us, and maybe we won't. But if we don't, we must understand that is not proof of God's cruelty or His non-existence.

This is a very difficult reality to accept, especially for Americans. We are a self-centered people. By that I don't mean to suggest that we aren't generous or charitable; just that we are used to getting what we want. And when we want answers from anyone, including God, we expect them. Actually, it's more than that...we feel we deserve them, and we deserve them NOW.

But the truth is that God is not obligated to give us any answers. It's totally God's prerogative to do things and allow things as He wishes, with or without making it clear to us. He's God and He can do what He wants. If that wasn't the case, He wouldn't be God.

A powerful portion of Francis Chan's book *Crazy Love* explains this well. It points out how Scripture tells us in Colossians 1:16 that everything was created for God. Not us. In other words, He's the center of the story and the focal point to everything. Not us. The Bible is full of this truth.

Psalm 115:3 reminds us that, "Our God is in heaven; He does whatever pleases Him." So if that's God's place, then what about us? Daniel 4:35 puts us in our place: "And the peoples of the earth are regarded as nothing. He does as He pleases with the powers of heaven and the peoples of the earth. No one can hold back His hand or say to Him: 'What have you done?'"

Yet, is that not exactly what we are attempting to say to Him when we shake our fist at the sky and demand God explain why He allows a child to suffer or a spouse to betray us? Are we not asking God, "What have you done?" Who do we think we are?

Sounds Like a Snake

Another uncomfortable reality we might want to notice is who we really sound like when we level the accusation of cruelty against God. Despite His promise to us that He loves us, we nonetheless peg God as a liar and slander His motive. Does that not sound like the serpent in the Garden of Eden? He told Eve that: 1. She wouldn't die if she ate the fruit even though God told her she would – in other words, God is a liar. And 2. The reason God didn't want her to eat the fruit wasn't because He was concerned for her, but because He knew she'd become as strong and wise as He was – in other words, God's motives are impure and dishonest.

Call me crazy, but I really don't think we're on

solid theological or rational grounds if the best we can
muster is the pathetic sniveling of Satan a few thousand
years post-Eden.

Besides, just follow the accusation through
logically and realize how unsound it is. Let's assume
for the sake of argument that the character of God is
defined by pathological cruelty. If that is the true
personality of God, it should be what we experience of
Him regularly, should it not? But that's not what we
experience at all. With few exceptions, the testimony of
the human race reveals lives filled with pleasure and
joy with sporadic challenges of pain. This reality
simply isn't compatible with the character of a sadist.

Irwin Linton explained it this way:

"[God] could give us infinitely more pain
than we do suffer. He could force us to eat as
the drug addict is forced to the use of his
drug, by the pain of abstention instead of by
the pleasing urge of healthy hunger. All the
physical functions could be forced by pain
instead of invited by pleasure...If God were
indifferent, why the variety of fruit flavors
for the palate, the invariably harmonizing
riot of colors in flower and sunset, the tang of
salt air and power to vibrate in joy in these
things?...If God loves His creatures all is
explained, except death, pain and sorrow,
and these things would indeed present, as
they do present to all BUT believers, an
insoluble problem. But the Bible's

explanation is clear as crystal: 'Death came
by sin,' and the glorious end is as succinctly
put as the explanation, 'And God shall wipe
all tears from their eyes.'"[5]

It's a fascinating point. So much of what we do as
humans is invited by the promise of pleasure, not the
fear or avoidance of pain. Think of eating. People love
to eat. They love the taste of their favorite foods. Why
would God give this immense pleasure to us if He were
inherently cruel by nature? Why not make eating a
painful experience, but one that was nonetheless
necessary for survival? "Go through the pain of eating
or die," would seem like a much crueler design than,
"You must eat, so I will make that a source of
enjoyment for you."

The same goes for reproduction, rest…virtually all
of our human experiences. Think about your life and
notice the daily blessings. Why the joy of holding your
infant child? Why the beautiful harmonies of music?
Why the ocean sunsets? Are these blessings the
handiwork of a cruel deity? To the contrary, when
viewed from a wide lens, the human experience is
powerful evidence against the idea of a sadistic God.

No One is Good

All of this doesn't eliminate the reality of pain or
sorrow, of course. Suffering is unquestionably part of
the human life, and some lives seem particularly
challenged by hardship. By that I am not referring to
those who choose dangerous or deadly lives of crime. I

mean those who through seemingly no fault of their own manage to stumble from one tragedy to the next. These are the stories that cause the age old question to permeate our thinking: "Why do bad things happen to good people?"

I can't tell you how many times I've been asked, or have pondered myself, that very question. Why does the drunk driver live, but the mother of four who is innocently and alertly driving home from the grocery store late one night perish? Why does the swindling adulterer live a life of privilege while an honest and loving family suffers immense grief? Why *do* bad things happen to good people? The truth is that the question itself actually betrays the faulty premise that explains our confusion.

Notice in the question that our default assumption is that we are good people, deserving of God's blessing. But that's not the truth of humanity. Scripture reminds us in Romans that only God is good: "There is no one righteous, not even one; All have turned away; there is no one who does good, not even one."[6]

Plain English? There is no human who can rightfully say that they are worthy of anything good. If we got what we deserve, we would receive eternal punishment. Now. If God is the ultimate standard of good, meaning that He defines what good is, then even the best among us falls woefully, pitifully short. We deserve to be wiped off the face of the earth for our sins and for the fact that every inclination and desire of our heart turns towards evil. That means that every second we live is only by the grace of God.

Therefore, our original question must be rephrased appropriately. Our question should never occasionally be, "Why do bad things happen to good people?" Instead, every day it should be, "Why does God give such good things to bad people like us?" That is the proper perspective.

The Big Picture

It seems cliché and empty to say after a tragedy has occurred, or in the midst of someone's suffering, that God will bring good from every situation. While it may be true, the statement itself seems a hollow reassurance and almost comes across as an attempt to diminish the real pain being experienced. Still, remembering our severely limited perspective in comparison to the infinite fullness of God's purpose is critical. James asks us, "What is your life? You are a mist that appears for a little while and then vanishes."[7]

That obviously doesn't mean your life is not valuable or significant. Remember that to God, you were worth the life of His only Son. What it does mean is that life isn't about us and our circumstances. It's about God and His purposes. It's His story.

In *Crazy Love*, Chan asks his readers to imagine that they landed the role of an extra in an upcoming movie in which they appear on the screen for about 2/5ths of a second. He describes it as the kind of role where it would be nearly impossible to pause the movie and actually catch your face on the screen.

He challenges his readers to imagine going around telling everyone you are the star of such a movie, even renting out the theater for opening night. No one would even see you and they'd think you're nuts. But Chan points out that such insanity is exactly how many of us humans think about our lives. We assume we're the star when the truth is that we're on the screen for 2/5ths of a second. It's not our movie, Chan reminds us. It's God's. He's the star.[8]

We don't know how our individual circumstances that God allows or disallows will be used to His ultimate purpose or glory. The truth is we don't have to. If we accept the reality of the infinite, eternal God, who exists outside of our space and time, His ways are sometimes beyond comprehension, and we will never fully understand them. While that may seem depressing at first, the truth is that it offers a peace that is liberating. It offers us the opportunity to put full trust in God's will.

I remember hearing a fairly well circulated anecdote about a farmer who owned a horse. One day the horse ran away, and all the townspeople came to the farmer to express their sadness over his loss. The farmer just said, "Oh I don't know…maybe it's a bad thing, maybe it's not. Time will tell."

Less than a week later, the horse returned to the farm along with 20 other horses…he'd gone into the wild and made friends. The townspeople all came to the farmer to congratulate him on his new, full stable of horses. The farmer just said, "Oh I don't know…maybe it's a good thing, maybe it's not. Time will tell."

A few days later, the farmer's only son was out riding one of the new horses that had come to the farm. Not well trained the horse became spooked and threw the farmer's son off, breaking both of his legs. All the townspeople came to the farmer to console him because of the injury to his son. The farmer just said, "Oh I don't know…maybe it's a bad thing, maybe it's not. Time will tell."

It wasn't a week later that the government declared war and instituted a necessary draft of all able-bodied young men. Officials came to the town and carted off hundreds of young men – except the farmer's young son who had two broken legs. It was at that point, with relief in his heart, that the farmer got on his knees and thanked God his horse had run away.

Here's the critical conclusion we must accept, whether it is easy or not. Sometimes our human experience allows us to eventually see God's ultimate provision and wisdom through difficult circumstances, like it did for that farmer. But sometimes it doesn't. Just because it doesn't, in no way empowers or justifies us using the temporary suffering of our vaporous few years of existence to render some authoritative judgment on the goodness of God's eternal purposes.

God is good because He told us He is.

7

"GOD SET US UP TO FAIL"

The Challenge

At the outset God made this into a life-and-death situation. God staked the entire future of mankind on this one event. We lost. The moment that Adam and Eve ate that fruit, wheels were set in motion that would ultimately result in the doom of mankind. Without some kind of intervention from God we would all be damned.

God does promise to intervene, but it's like building a nuclear bomb and setting it to go off in a large city at 12:00. Then, when all of the people of the city come to you for mercy, you disarm it for them. Does that make you a hero for disarming it or a lunatic for building it in the first place? The whole thing was orchestrated to make us feel dependent upon God. That says a lot about God's character.[1]

- Daniel Pock

Where Would This Leave Us?

In determining whether God is some kind of psychotic who just set us up to fail, we once again find ourselves in the uncomfortable philosophical position of trying to judge the morality of God based on our own sense of morality – an intellectual and logical minefield to be sure. Nonetheless, it is important to fully understand that this allegation is very similar to what we just finished addressing. It is another attack on the goodness and loving nature of God.

The argument goes that the Garden of Eden was the seminal moment of truth, where the fate of all things hung in the balance. God placed Adam and Eve there, and with willful intent handed them over to the deception of the serpent. The unspoken assumption is that obviously Adam and Eve were no match for the cunning of the serpent, who seduced and manipulated these two innocent individuals, sealing their – and our – eternal doom.

Then, victims of God's cruel set-up, we watch Him descend on the scene and play the role of hero, offering mercy through Jesus. The argument encourages us to not fall for God's manipulation, recognizing that He is the wacko that started the whole mess in the first place.

I have to admit that I've always been a bit confused by this argument because of where it would leave us. Think about it. Suppose this whole scenario really is true, just as the skeptic describes it. If God truly were that deranged, sitting in heaven and manipulating us towards a doomsday we have no power to resist, what exactly is the point in complaining about it? Could we gain anything by coming to this conclusion? If we uncovered that we're all pawns in God's cruel plot, would we be in any better position to stop it? Of course not. If anything, we'd have more reason than ever to be depressed, bitter and angry. That's why I will never fully understand the sense of pleasure so many skeptics get in promoting this theory. If they really believed what they were saying, smug satisfaction is the last emotion they would exude.

Nevertheless, this remains one of the more common lines of attack utilized by those seeking to justify their rebellion to God. And the truth is that the argument trips up more Christians than it should. Seriously, I am amazed at how compelling and concerning we believers find this accusation, given how overrun it is with generalizations, oversimplifications, understatements and overstatements. Let me explain just a few of them.

Mistake One: Assuming the Motive

One of the most common errors perpetrated in logical debate is assuming a motive without actual proof. The truth is that as we dive into these kinds of questions like, "Why would God go ahead with the world even when He saw it falling apart?" or "It sure seems like God set us up to fail," we may not find answers that totally satisfy us.

But not having an answer does not allow us to draw a conclusion one way or the other. Absence of an answer does not prove that God is the psychotic that the skeptic suggests He is. If we don't know why God did things the way He did, that doesn't mean God did them for the reason the skeptic said He did. It simply means we are left ignorant of the answer. Drawing a conclusion based on ignorance is...well, ignorant.

Mistake Two: Missing Information

It's important to remember that Genesis is a record of what God knew we needed to know about the beginning. We needed to know about His creative power. We needed to know about our sin and the fact that it brought death into the world. We needed to know what death was the punishment for and when it entered the world. But Genesis isn't a comprehensive study of everything that occurred in the Garden. The skeptic's challenge here doesn't take that into account.

Glenn Miller posits a number of questions that help explain what I mean. Would it change the dynamics of the situation to you if you knew that maybe Adam and Eve had resisted the serpent 10 times or 100 times before they finally gave in? Or maybe that Adam and Eve lived in obedience to God in the Garden for 100 years before the fall? Or maybe the other animals in the Garden were crafty too, and participated in the trickery? Or maybe that God's act of punishment was also an act of mercy – because allowing fallen and sinful humans to eat from the Tree of Life would have guaranteed them an eternity of suffering and toil? Or maybe there's a reason there is no mention of Hell or even anger and wrath in this passage? Or maybe there's a reason that man and woman didn't die the instant they ate the fruit, and maybe that reason has to do with God's goodness? Or maybe God's reaction would have been different if Adam and Eve would have sought God out with an honest and repentant confession after sinning?[2]

Now, please understand that I am not implying anything theological or otherwise with those questions. I don't know the answer to any of them. And that's the whole point. We have very little information about the scene in the Garden, so constructing wild theories about God's motivations from this small passage is anti-intellectual and beyond speculative. Of course, that's exactly what you would expect when a created being attempts to sit in judgment of his Creator.

At its heart, you can already begin to see what this challenge to God's goodness is at best: a thinly supported conspiracy theory based on unreliable and wild conjecture and assumption.

Mistake Three: Helpless Humans

Let's also acknowledge the stunning fact that the skeptic totally eliminates man from the whole equation, absolving him from any responsibility whatsoever. The assumption is that once Adam sinned, the whole thing was spring loaded like a bear trap, snapping shut on billions of innocent humans who would follow –

through absolutely no fault of their own. This is the fallacy of determinism; a washed up theory that assumes no role for free will, moral choices, or personal autonomy in God's universe.

But the notion of man and woman being helpless robots in the Garden, merely acting out a cruel drama without possessing any individual ability to deviate from the script, simply doesn't fit with the complex character of conscious choice human beings have and exhibit every day.

Anyone who buys into this fatalistic theory should be very wary, because the implications of their beliefs are gravely serious. The opinion that God orchestrated everything to happen the way He desired means that all decisions by man are merely whatever God wills them to be. So that means man really doesn't have a will, and there is really only one will in the entire universe: God's. But if that's the case, the introduction of sin into the world must have come about because God desired it, meaning there can only be one sinner in the universe: God. Ultimately then, you and I don't matter, and there's simply no reason to have this discussion.

But notice that we're having it. So thankfully, there must be more to it.

Mistake Four: Superior Snake

In the skeptic's scenario, we are apparently to believe that the temptation of the snake was too much for Adam and Eve, and God knew it. He abandoned them to a situation that He knew they'd never overcome. This is where the whole "set us up for failure" argument hinges. But it makes absolutely no sense to believe this given that it contradicts everything we see throughout the Bible. Scripture tells us God does not allow temptation beyond that which we can bear.[3] According to the New Testament, Satan (who took on the form of the serpent in the Garden) can be resisted by humans.[4]

Even in the Genesis account itself, the snake is placed just above the animals while Adam was set over all the animals. In other words, Adam, not the serpent, had the superiority.[5] Adam and Eve's son, Cain, was instructed by God to "master" sin,[6] and Job successfully overcame Satan's direct attacks.[7]

What does all this mean? It means that there is simply nothing beyond imagination and mindless speculation to conclude that Adam and Eve were in a helpless situation against the serpent. All contextual evidence tells us the exact opposite. And remember, we don't know if the serpent had been resisted by Adam and Eve multiple times before. We just don't have enough information to draw a conclusion like this.

Mistake Five: Choosing Our Hell

The idea that the future of mankind was staked on this one event in the Garden of Eden is a bit loaded and misleading. Don't get me wrong, the fallout of Genesis 3 is critical to understanding man's depravity and need for a savior. But what I mean is that Jesus Christ's redemptive work on the cross ensures that no man has to face the consequences of sin. Thus, the future state of our eternal soul is staked on our own choice – not Adam and Eve's.

If you doubt this point, here's a sampling of Scripture that reinforces this truth: the book of Jeremiah cautions, "Instead, everyone will die for their own sin; whoever eats sour grapes – their own teeth will be set on edge."[8]

In the same way, Matthew reminds us, "For the Son of Man is going to come in his Father's glory with his angels, and then he will reward each person according to what they have done."[9]

And the book of Revelation warns, "The dead were judged according to what they had done as recorded in the books."[10] These simple and straightforward lessons from Scripture completely undermine the false representation of reality perpetrated by the skeptic.

His challenge creates a scenario so twisted that it's tough to even make sense of it. Seriously…just try to: God provides us no choice but to fail, then punishes us for our choices – even though we don't really make choices. Of course, if we don't really make choices, we wouldn't be subject to Hell because we didn't do anything deserving punishment. And while we're at it, if moral choices don't really matter, then why are we criticizing God for making a supposedly immoral choice?[11]

If you're thoroughly confused right now, don't bother going back and re-reading that paragraph – it won't help. You can't make sense of that maze of inanity even with the assistance of star charts. Yet, that is the logical mess the skeptic has created for himself trying to assail the character of God.

Scripture tells us that Hell is matched directly to the actions and works of the one being punished, because the point of Hell is judgment and justice, not the final bizarre act in God's deluded drama.

Mistake Six: Bomb Backwardness

I will admit that the first time I read the nuclear bomb analogy posed by the skeptic, it gave me pause. In fact, it did more than that. It bothered me. A lot. Because the first time I read it, my human nature caused me to respond emotionally. And eliciting emotional responses, I might add, is precisely the objective of the skeptic. He is merely seeking to incite a negative emotional reaction to the goodness of God. Because without thinking critically about what was being argued, my emotions convinced me it was a far more compelling and intimidating argument than what it truly is.

But the second and third time I read it – and really started *thinking* about it – I began noticing some of the bizarre misrepresentations and backwards parallels that characterized any attempt to analogize

Eden to an act of terrorism. The scene of a madman
setting a nuclear bomb in a city is not even close to
being compatible with God placing Adam and Eve in
the lap of perfection. Yes, the consequences of man's
sin in that Garden – sin that we already established was
not God's intent or purpose – led to death. But saying
God wanted it so, or that He was the mastermind who
orchestrated an elaborate scheme to trap man, is to
deny all the information we have of Him.

So is there a better analogy to use that would
more accurately describe what really occurred there in
the Garden of Eden? How about this: God designs a
beautiful city full of rivers and gardens and streams.
Buildings are immaculate, elevators run smoothly,
walkways are clean, grass is well groomed, windows
are spotless, traffic runs perfectly. He puts everything
in place for man to live in splendor and pleasure. But
the men who live there eventually corrupt the city,
splitting it into rival gangs. Those gangs come into
possession of nuclear weapons which they plant and
begin their doomsday countdown. Watching the mess
they are making with great sadness and
disappointment, God intervenes, constructing and
offering a second city – even better than the first – to
those who recognize and confess the impending doom
they have brought on themselves.[12] A bit different
picture of God emerges from this more accurate
analogy, doesn't it?

Mistake Seven: Pass the Buck

The skeptic's entire scenario is designed to make

it seem that man bears no responsibility and that it's all God's fault. The intent is to force us to reconsider how we could worship a God who saved us from what He did to us in the first place. Implicit in that challenge is the absurd proposition that God had no right to create us, and then expect us to follow certain moral guidelines and standards.

Glenn Miller responds with a real life analogy to demonstrate how silly this is:

> "Let's say that I am a member of a tribe, and that we all meet together and decide that it would be against our best interests to allow members of the tribe to sneak up on other members of the tribe while they are asleep and kill them, in order to take all their possessions. And then we decide that if someone does that crime, they will subsequently be whipped and executed in front of the others, to reinforce the seriousness of the need for trustworthy relationships among the tribe.
>
> Now let's say I commit such a crime – I kill my neighbor and move all his belongings into my hut. When I am found out, the tribe's tribunal finds me guilty and sentences me to death for my crime. I weep and wail, beg and plead, and eventually – somehow – convince them to spare my life and that I will never, ever violate the law of the tribe and betray the community trust again.

When I accept their pardon for my crime,
would it make any sense for me to discount
that because 'they pardoned me from
something they set up in the first place?' Of
course not – the rules that were 'set up' were
for good. That I was sentenced to
punishment was not the fault of the rules, but
of my disregard for them. I cannot shift the
blame to some 'system' – or worse, to the
system creator – when it simply operates
efficiently."[13]

In other words, all Adam and Eve had to do was
listen to God and obey Him, and there would have
never been a negative consequence. They did not need
to eat from the Tree of the Knowledge of Good and Evil
because they already possessed moral and ethical
discernment in its perfect form: trusting God to tell
them what was right and wrong. But they rebelled,
and faced the consequences. That is their fault, not
God's.

It's worthwhile to note that the skeptic is blaming
God for what happened in the Garden, which is exactly
what Adam and Eve did. First, Adam blamed God for
putting Eve there to lure him into her mistakes.[14] Then
Eve blamed God for putting the serpent there to trick
her.[15] Several thousand years later, it's nice to see that
human nature hasn't changed one bit.

Of course, it's not just human nature that has
remained constant over that time. The character of God
has as well. And that's the last point to note. In the

final analysis, if God really was this malevolent and nefarious to orchestrate the scenario presented by the skeptic, our experience with Him in this life should reflect that reality. But as we discussed earlier in the book, that just simply isn't the case. Not even close.

Judging the Motive

Remember what we said at the outset of this chapter: we may not end with an answer that provides us certainty why God allowed the serpent to tempt, or why God gave us the free will to disobey Him. But looking at the evidence we have been provided, we *can* have certainty to say this about the skeptic:

1. He makes outrageous assumptions without sufficient information in Scripture.
2. He greatly oversimplifies the complexity of free will.
3. He draws outlandish conclusions about the power and influence of Satan.
4. He weaves an emotionally provocative, but intellectually backwards nuclear bomb analogy.
5. He overstates the impact that the fall of Adam and Eve had on your eternal fate and mine.
6. He attempts an extraordinarily reckless effort to pass the buck of responsibility.
7. In the final analysis, he produces nothing more with this challenge than a thinly disguised conspiracy theory based solely on speculation, assumption and conjecture.

So even if we couldn't draw a conclusive answer about God's motive, we can certainly draw one about our skeptic's. This is not an earnest attempt to discover more about our Creator, it's an attempt to slander Him.

The character of a bomb-setting, moral choice-denying, controlling, manipulative megalomaniac is as far from the character of the Biblical God as the east is from the west.

8

"GOD CONDONES SLAVERY"

The Challenge

"Except for murder, slavery has got to be one of the most immoral things a person can do. Yet slavery is rampant throughout the Bible in both the Old and New Testaments. The Bible clearly approves of slavery in many passages, and it goes so far as to tell how to obtain slaves, how hard you can beat them, and when you can have sex with the female slaves...

So these are the Bible family values! A man can buy as many sex slaves as he wants as long as he feeds them, clothes them, and screws them!

What does the Bible say about beating slaves? It says you can beat both male and female slaves with a rod so hard that as long as they don't die right away you are cleared of any wrong doing...

You would think that Jesus and the New Testament would have a different view of slavery, but slavery is still approved of in the New Testament."[1]   - *Chris Thiefe*

Ignoring the Bible

Some people will refer to them as the uncomfortable or even the embarrassing parts of Scripture. Whether they are references to bizarre sexual practices, commands to wipe out evil civilizations and the seemingly innocent people living in them, or in this case, the references to slavery, there are parts of the Bible that Christians often want to move past quickly.

Preachers gloss over them, church small groups ignore them, Sunday School classes dance around them whenever they come up. Seriously, when is the last time you heard a sermon on the Bible's teaching regarding slavery?

It shouldn't surprise us that the very topics that make Christians the most uncomfortable to talk about just happen to be the ones skeptics are most interested in discussing. And certainly in our current culture, nothing would seem to prove the Bible more antiquated, out of date, or even backwards and corrupt, as its references and seeming acceptance of slavery.

During a profanity-laced tirade where he mocked, chastised and attempted to humiliate Christian kids in attendance, homosexual sex columnist Dan Savage argued that Biblical condemnations of homosexuality should be ignored since, "We have learned to ignore the bulls*** in the Bible about...slavery."

He went on to assert that, "The Bible is a radically pro-slavery document," before launching into this concluding rant:

> "The shortest book in the New Testament is a letter from Paul to a Christian slave owner about owning his Christian slave. And Paul doesn't say, 'Christians don't own people.' Paul talks about how Christians own people. We ignore what the Bible says about slavery because the Bible got slavery wrong."[2]

Though Savage is factually incorrect about Philemon (the book he is referencing) being the shortest book in the New Testament since both 2 John and 3 John are shorter, is he right about his general thesis? Is this proof that there are at least parts of the Bible that we should ignore – or even oppose as immoral?

Or are the references to slavery not what he and other scoffers make them out to be? Once again, the Christian Think Tank offers some keen insights and research that helps us confront this hostile accusation from men like Savage.

Apples and Oranges?

The first thing that is absolutely critical to grasp is that when we hear the word slavery today, there are certain connotations that immediately come to our mind's eye.

We remember this country's sin of enslaving Africans, the brutal and inhuman treatment they were forced to suffer, the heart-wrenching separation that families experienced as slave auctioneers literally tore black children from the clutches of their wailing mothers. With that as our perspective, obviously any book or text that could or would condone such behavior should be considered immediately suspect.

But as tempting as it might be, we cannot automatically assume that the word slavery conjured up the same imagery or meant the same thing for New Testament Christian writers like Paul as it does for us today.

We know for certain that Old Testament era slavery was nothing even remotely similar to our modern understanding of the word. That fact is so widely known that in intellectual and scholarly circles, no one even makes the attempt to draw moral equivalence between the two. The relationship between slave and master in the Old Testament is remarkably more similar to a business relationship – with the obvious exceptions of say, the Egyptian enslavement of Israel.

But what about the slavery of the New Testament era practiced by the Romans? This is what surrounded the New Testament writers like Paul. So in order to cast judgment upon the Bible's treatment of slavery, intellectual honesty demands that we deduce these three things:

1. Was New Testament slavery compatible or incompatible with our modern understanding of slavery?

2. What should the Christian response to the slavery experienced in Roman times have been?

3. What was the teaching of the New Testament writers on the subject, and does that match what it should have been?

Answering these three questions will tell us whether the Bible, and therefore Christianity, really condones slavery as it is alleged.

Is New Testament Slavery Like Modern Slavery?

The quick answer to the question of whether the slavery seen in New Testament times was like the slavery of more modern times is no. Not even close. And, in fact, the areas where you see the most substantial difference between the two institutions just so happens to be the most concerning parts of modern slavery – things like the abuse, compulsion and discrimination.

Perhaps the easiest thing to do is to break up the topic of slavery into five categories, comparing and contrasting the New Testament era to early America to see just how different they are.

Purpose

For slave owners in early America, the motivation to own slaves was clear: it was an engine for economic prosperity. After the invention of the cotton gin, the desire to harvest larger and larger crops became insatiable. Slaves were desired for the expressed purpose of hard labor. Their exploitation meant great financial dividends for their masters.

New Testament era slavery was far less about economics, and far more about status. The more servants (a better descriptor for us to use in our modern lexicon) you had, the more prestigious you were perceived. In other words, your peers viewed you in a better light if you had someone else turning down your bed sheets for you. New Testament era slave owners were looking for comforts, service and to impress their friends, not to get wealthy.[3]

Treatment

All you have to do is read Harriet Beecher Stowe's *Uncle Tom's Cabin* to catch a glimpse of the kind of treatment slaves received in early America. If relentless, unending, back breaking manual labor weren't enough, many times those slaves would be whipped and beaten for poor performance.

And let's not forget their squalid living

conditions, where large slave families would be crowded into small cabins or leaky huts somewhere out of eyeshot on the sprawling plantation.

By contrast, the best way to picture New Testament era slaves is that of household servants, like butlers, maids, masseuses, or cooks. That's not to say there weren't field laborers. These types of slaves existed, and were often times prisoners put to work for their crimes. But by law, slaves were afforded far more creature comforts than what we would be tempted to think.

It's also important to note that contrary to the whipped-for-bad-performance model of American slaves, New Testament era slavery saw an incentive system for good performance. High performing slaves could sometimes make lots of money, including livestock and property, for their excellence.

And in terms of their living conditions, most slaves shared in the residence of their masters. They lived in surroundings of wealth and prestige, sleeping under the same roof as the remainder of the household.[4]

Social Status

This is a jaw-dropping distinction between the two models of slavery we are discussing. In early America, slaves were undeniably poor and destitute. They had no hope or opportunity of advancing out of their miserable state, and were beings to be pitied for their plight.

Not so in the New Testament era, where there were actually social classes within the world of the slave. The lowest slaves could best be described as sharecroppers, working the land and sharing the crop that was raised. But slaves did not need to stay at that level, and the truth is that few did. Some slaves made so much money and owned so much property that the term "slave elite" was coined to describe them.

The notion of a "wealthy slave" would be an oxymoron when viewed through our cultural lens today. But the phrase is commonplace in ancient texts of this New Testament time period. In fact, the possibility of attaining very high levels of power and status as a slave in the right households caused many men of average means to sell themselves into slavery for a shot at advancement.[5]

I don't think I have to tell you that the image of men competing with each other to land a job as a slave is certainly not the picture of the institution most modern Americans possess. It was, however, the picture of the institution New Testament writers would have held.

Legal Recourse

It's pretty simple to sum up the legal options for slaves in early America: none. Just ask Dred Scott.

Slaves were considered legal property and therefore couldn't sue, couldn't own assets or enter into legal contracts. Meanwhile, there were few (if any) real limitations put upon their masters.

That's why this is the area of biggest difference with New Testament era slavery. Slaves in Roman days could own property, take out loans, and enter into binding agreements or contracts. They could bring litigation and, if they so desired, represent themselves in court.

There was even a legal means for slaves to sue for their freedom, or to gain a transfer to a different master. Sometimes a slave could simply flee to an image of the emperor in order to obtain a transfer – it was that simple.

Further, Roman law held masters strictly accountable for the treatment of slaves. Consider that while the law allowed masters to promote their slaves above their own familial heirs in the master's will, it greatly restricted his ability to "demote" slaves from the position they held.

Additionally, Roman slaves could easily file complaints with the courts about treatment, and many times the courts sided with the slaves over the masters.[6]

Needless to say, any fair observer would notice that the distinctions between early American and New Testament era slavery are growing immense.

Escape

Finally, the notion of how the enslaved escaped their condition. For slaves in early America, attempting to escape meant breaking the law and risking your life. Unless their conditions were unbearable, many decided the attempt was simply not worth the risk. Because the sad truth was that even if the initial escape attempt was successful, there existed the continual threat of being recaptured and either sent back or re-sold.

And let's not overlook the sad reality that since these slaves lacked money, property or the formal education to earn either for themselves, successful escape did not necessarily improve their condition.

None of this was the case for New Testament era slaves during Roman times. The practice of manumission – the intentional freeing of slaves by masters – was expected in early Roman culture, and usually happened around the time of the slave's 30th birthday. Not only would the slave be free, but they were immediately granted Roman citizenship, meaning there was no fear of being returned to slavery against their will.

Manumission occurred so regularly and frequently, there were actually some laws written to restrict the amount of slaves that were manumitted at once.

From a broad perspective, the Roman legal structure historically favored the granting of freedom over the retention of slaves. Yet incredibly, the economic status and prestige of being a slave in an upper class household was so alluring, many chose that lifestyle over the plentiful options before them to attain freedom and strike out on their own.[7]

So clearly these two systems are night and day, black and white, polar opposites. So much so that we poison the well of debate by referring to both institutions by the same word. We shouldn't. They are that different.

What that means is that if our purpose is to judge the morality or immorality of New Testament Christian teachings about slavery, it is absolutely necessary that we look at the institution through the appropriate prism.

We are not talking about the greed-centered, abuse-laden, racial superiority struggle of the New World Americas. What we are talking about is a status-driven servant-hood that was often times chosen, not compelled, and that offered legal recourse and opportunities for economic and physical escape.

Once we stand on that solid ground, we can fairly answer our second question.

What Should the Christian Response Have Been?

In trying to give a direct response to what the Christian teaching should have been regarding New

Testament era slavery, an intellectually honest person finds themselves in a dilemma.

Unlike early America slavery that can definitively be labeled "always wrong," the situation with New Testament Roman slavery is different. The institution there, as we've seen, was so varied that you almost have to render judgment solely on a case by case basis.

But generally speaking, here are five basic expectations that a Christian treatment of the kind of slavery we have just described should fulfill:

1. We should see a teaching against the slave trade since it was involuntary.

2. We should see condemnation of abuse of slaves by masters, and also condemnation of disrespect of masters by slaves.

3. We should see correction of this idea of "classes" of people.

4. Given the complexity of this system, we shouldn't see a blanket call to free all slaves.

That one might make you a little curious until you do some research. When you do, you will discover that some of these Roman slaves were taken as infants, rescued by masters from exposure (a Roman-era form of after-birth abortion that involved abandoning infant children to die of malnutrition, the elements or animals). The master's provision was therefore all that stood between those "slaves" and death.

And this was true not just for infants. Other slaves were old or sick, and there was no welfare system outside of the early Christian Church to care for them. Some counts put the number of Roman slaves as high as 40% of the empire's total population, meaning that cultural chaos would have erupted if all of them had been "freed" instantly.

Many slaves would have suffered immensely from such a reality, losing everything (quite possibly including their lives) as a result.

That's the reality that the New Testament era writers were facing – a far more nuanced situation than the one facing Henry Ward Beecher, Frederick Douglass and Abraham Lincoln.

> 5. Finally, though a blanket admonition for abolition would have been imprudent, we should see a Christian appeal for masters to evaluate the conditions of their slaves, and if it would be for the slaves' good, make the conscience-driven decision to free them.[8]

That is what any moral scripture would say about New Testament era slavery. So then, what does the New Testament actually say?

What Does the New Testament Say About Slavery?

First, we immediately see a condemnation of the slave trade. Paul clearly lumps slave traders in with adulterers, perverts, liars and perjurers, claiming their actions are contrary to sound doctrine.[9]

Second, abuse by masters and disrespect by slaves is condemned. Masters are told to give up threatening[10] and to grant slaves justice and fairness.[11] In those same passages, slaves are instructed to be obedient with sincerity, and to in all things obey as though they are serving the Lord, not men. This theme is repeated in Titus where slaves are warned against stealing and being argumentative.[12]

Third, the idea of different "classes" of people is rebuked and corrected. While the Jewish Pharisees referred to the slave class as "despised," the former Pharisee turned Christian Apostle Paul confirms the equal nature of slave and master under the Lordship of Christ, both in his letters to the Galatians[13] and the Colossians.[14]

Fourth, we don't see any top-down, blanket call to set all slaves free. Paul does condemn the slave trade, tells free men not to become slaves just to try to advance their social standing,[15] instructs slaves to seek their freedom,[16] and encourages Philemon to free his slave. But he avoids making any all-encompassing command for immediate abolition.

Fifth, we see a Christian admonition to make the conscience-driven decision to free slaves. In Philemon, Paul stresses repeatedly to the slave owner that he should free his slaves.[17] It's instructive why Paul writes that such an action is what Philemon ought to do, but doesn't directly command it. This approach isn't due to any ambivalence on Paul's part towards the issue, but rather out of a desire that Philemon act out of love and be blessed for it, rather than simply do it out of a begrudging obligation.[18]

Where Slavery Is No More

In answering our original three questions, we have stood the accusation that the Bible (or New Testament Christianity) condones slavery on its head.

First, New Testament era slavery was nothing like what we think of today. Second and third, exactly what we would and should expect Scripture to teach about the institution of slavery as it existed then, is exactly what it does teach.

The New Testament clearly advises the church to move away from the slave system, and it outright condemns the very elements of slavery that we find abhorrent and reprehensible: compulsion, oppression, mistreatment, discrimination towards certain groups of people, and racism.

It's not surprising, then, that unlike so many places in the world still suffering under the weight of slavery, Western culture that has been heavily influenced by New Testament Christianity has eliminated the institution entirely. And, though it would confound men like Dan Savage, we have used the Bible as our justification in eliminating it.

That fact is no coincidence.

9

"GOD COMMITTED GENOCIDE"

The Challenge

"The God of the Old Testament is arguably the most unpleasant character in all fiction: jealous and proud of it; a petty, unjust, unforgiving control-freak; a vindictive, bloodthirsty ethnic cleanser; a misogynistic, homophobic, racist, infanticidal, genocidal, filicidal, pestilential, megalomaniacal, sadomasochistic, capriciously malevolent bully. Those of us schooled from infancy in his ways can become desensitized to their horror."[1]   *- Richard Dawkins*

A Schizophrenic God?

It's always a question that surfaces in the Bible Literacy class I teach at the public high school where I work. As we read through the Old Testament pages that detail how the Israelites take possession of the

Promised Land (or "Land of Canaan"), there are some pretty brutal battle scenes that provoke a response. For instance, take this passage from Deuteronomy that always raises a few eyebrows:

> "However, in the cities of the nations the LORD your God is giving you as an inheritance, do not leave alive anything that breathes. Completely destroy them — the Hittites, Amorites, Canaanites, Perizzites, Hivites and Jebusites — as the LORD your God has commanded you."[2]

Now, it's not that the passage is overly graphic or grotesque, particularly for young people who are routinely exposed to far more violent imagery in movies and video games. But what gives them pause is the fact that these acts of violence are being endorsed and required by a supposedly all-merciful God. As a result, I can be guaranteed that I will take at least one question that asks, "Why would God order such a complete destruction of people? Doesn't that include innocent women and children?"

It's a great question, and an increasingly popular one amongst those who seek to challenge the goodness of God. It won't take too long after engaging a skeptic before they will point to some of the events of the Old Testament and say, "Do you see what your God did or commanded?" They highlight as many examples of brutality or violence in the history of the Old Testament as they can, and suggest that such behavior simply is not compatible with a God of love, mercy and grace.

And all too often, in a feeble attempt to deflect this line of attack, Christians will say things like, "Well, that was the Old Testament. But God is different now. His behavior in the New Testament is where we experience His love." This defense makes it seem as though God wasn't loving in the Old Testament, and isn't just in the New Testament. I actually heard one lady say that the difference in God can be explained because He had a kid. "Once you have children, you see things differently," she said. Not to belittle her creativity and imagination, but...no. No, that's not right. Not even close. Hebrews tells us that God's character is changeless, the same yesterday, today and forever.[3] And we should be ever grateful for that truth.

Because suppose it were true that spontaneously and without provocation, God decided to alter His character from wrath and vengeance to love and mercy. That would suggest a volatile, moody, unpredictable or even schizophrenic God – meaning He is completely unreliable and capable of changing His attitude towards us at any time, for any reason. No, the unchanging, fixed character of God is one of His most awesome qualities.

But that means we can't and shouldn't just brush away these questions about alleged Old Testament slaughter. Is God a genocidal maniac who willfully ordered the massacre of people – innocent people – simply because they weren't his chosen favorites?

Observation One: Few Examples

The first thing we should notice when we start combing the Scriptures is how few examples there really are of this alleged slaughter-happy genocide. Now certainly, one true genocide is enough to call into question the character of the one who orders it, so we aren't going to just blow it off. But the point remains that for the thousands and thousands of years of history that the Old Testament encompasses, we really only find four significant examples of this alleged brutality of God: Sodom & Gomorrah, The Flood of Noah, the Amalekites, and the Canaanites (sometimes called the Amorites).

If you're glancing back at that passage from Deuteronomy and saying, "Uh, what about the Jebusites, Hivites, Perrizites, and the others?" remember that these were all nations living throughout the land of Canaan – the land God promised to Israel. So in the Old Testament books of conquest, there are specific accounts of how Israel defeated particular nations or tribes in the land of Canaan. But since they all are part of God's same command to take possession of this land, there's no need to treat them individually. We can use "Canaanite" as the umbrella grouping for all of them.

So again, before we go any further, just step back and consider this logically. If God were truly a blood thirsty, malevolent Being that delighted in seeing His creation embroiled in the brutality of war, wouldn't we expect to see more of it in thousands of years than just four examples? Though it's pretty clear something isn't adding up with this accusation, it's still important to dig a little deeper and look at the examples themselves. Is this really genocide?

Observation Two: A Predictable Pattern

Our friend Glenn Miller has done much of the legwork for us in observing and documenting a distinct pattern that is present in each of these four "slaughter" examples:

1. The destruction is always a judgment of God for crimes, never arbitrary or unprovoked action.

2. The crimes of the destroyed people are not subjective. They are extreme, widespread cruelty, perversion and violence known throughout the world.

3. The destruction comes only after long periods of warning and opportunity to change.

4. Innocent adults are always given a way out.

5. Children always share the fate of their parents – sometimes that ends with their safety, sometimes their demise.

6. Somebody always escapes.[4]

If this is accurate, it completely obliterates any notion that these commands of God are morally equivalent with genocide. In fact, is a repeated call to repent, long periods of patience followed by swift judgment for persistent and violent disobedience, always accompanied by the truly innocent surviving, not precisely the action we would expect from a loving, good and just God?

Let's look at the four examples specifically to see if Miller is right and if the skeptic's accusation falls flat.

Sodom and Gomorrah

The book of Genesis details how the people of Sodom and Gomorrah inhabited a good land and were exposed to righteousness both through the witness of Abraham and Melchizedek the priest. Despite this, the people chose to participate in outright evil, committing heinous crimes against God and each other. For 25 years God was patient, as Lot witnessed and attempted to set an example for them of righteous, Godly living.

Eventually, the sin became so excessive that people throughout the area cried out to God for deliverance, at which point He sends angels to destroy the city. But even then, upon hearing the pleas of Abraham, God agrees to spare the city if only 10 righteous people can be found. Yet the evil of the city was so great (Scripture records that, "*All* the men from every part of the city of Sodom — both young and old — surrounded the house"[5] to sexually assault the angels staying with Lot) that only Lot and his family were found to be worthy of rescue. So God destroyed the city and surrounding area, swiftly and completely.

Does this account fit the Miller pattern? 1. It was certainly an act of judgment for crimes. 2. The crimes were immense and known internationally. 3. The destruction came after at least 25 years of calls to change. 4. God offered to spare any innocents who were found. 5. Children shared the fate of their parents. 6. The one innocent man and his family were spared (a case where children share the fate of their parents for good).[6]

The Flood of Noah

We know this story pretty well. God's heart is grieved by the evil He sees, but He decides to spare the innocent man Noah and his family (here again, notice the consistency of God, as children share the fate of their parents for good or ill). God tells Noah to build an Ark. While building, Noah draws a lot of attention and uses that time to preach righteousness to the people. This went on for 100 years – four guys building a boat three stories high and the length of almost two football fields didn't happen overnight. Yet despite Noah's teaching, Genesis records that the people were overcome with evil and committed wicked acts against God and against each other.[7] So God destroyed the earth, completely and swiftly.

Does this account, like Sodom and Gomorrah, fit the Miller pattern? 1. It was certainly an act of judgment for crimes. 2. The crimes were immense and worldwide. 3. The destruction came after at least 100 years of calls to change. 4. God was willing to spare the innocent, if there were any. 5. Children share the fate of their parents. 6. The one innocent man and his family were spared.[8]

The Amalekites

The Amalekites were descendants of Esau. If you don't remember your Old Testament history very well, Esau was the jilted brother of Jacob (Jacob was also known as Israel, and his sons headed the various tribes of that chosen nation). The sibling rivalry between Jacob and Esau had transcended generations, so the Amalekites (Esau's descendants) were quite familiar with and held a real grudge against Israel (Jacob's descendants). These Amalekite nomads spent most of their time wandering around the area south of the Promised Land, attacking and raiding whoever they could find.

The reason that's significant is because as Israel completed the Exodus from Egypt and made their way to the Promised Land, the Amalekites would have been out of their way and in no danger. But harboring the resentment of previous generations, when the Amalekites heard that Israel was on the march out of Egypt, they made a special effort to find them and attack them.

By the way, as a quick side note, notice that despite all their crimes (including the enslavement and mistreatment of God's people for hundreds of years),

Egypt was not destroyed by God, but only punished. Call me crazy, but that's certainly not what I would expect from a genocidal God.

Anyway, besides being vicious marauders, this incident makes it fair to say that the Amalekites weren't very bright either. After seeing God's miraculous hand of providence deliver Israel from Egypt, the Amalekites thought it would be a good idea to make the long journey just to pick a fight.

And Scripture makes it clear they didn't just attack. They specifically targeted Israel's helpless and most vulnerable, both the old and the sick.[9] Given this background, you would have expected a swift and harsh response from Israel. But that apparently didn't happen, as the Amalekites would continue these attacks and raids for roughly three centuries. After what can only be described as remarkable tolerance and restraint, God's patience eventually runs out and the destruction is ordered.

So did it fit the Miller pattern? 1. It was certainly an act of judgment. 2. The crimes were numerous and immense. 3. The destruction came after at least 400 years since they knew God promised Israel this land. And remember, they had watched God's work to save Israel from Egypt, so they knew what they were getting themselves into before they attacked. 4. God attempted to save all the innocent, even sending Saul to announce before the judgment that all the blameless Kenites, "Move away so that I do not destroy you along with them."[10] 5. Children shared the fate of their parents. 6.

The innocent Kenites and repentant Amalekites who fled were spared, along with their families.[11]

The Canaanites

Finally, we come to the people that always seem to draw the most questions: the Canaanites. To a casual observer, it just sounds unfair – God handpicks one group of people He likes best and then tells the others to get out of the way or be slaughtered. But in order to investigate and discover whether God really is a genocidal maniac, we have to be more than just casual observers.

One of the first things to note is that in Genesis 15, God specifically tells Abraham that his descendants – the children of Israel – will not be able to take the land until the sins of the Canaanites become really bad.[12] Already we can see that this doesn't sound like genocide. And evidence against the skeptic's accusation continues to mount when we discover who these Canaanite people really were, and what they were doing.

In actuality, we get the best and clearest picture of the Canaanites from extra-Biblical (or non-Biblical) sources. And what we find is that they were an extremely violent, bloodthirsty people who, after mercilessly slaughtering the kingdoms that had occupied the land before them, maintained an insatiable warlike obsession.

Not surprisingly, they were often times brutal to

each other, and engaged in some exceedingly vile and disgusting sexual and religious practices, including religiously accepted prostitution, homosexuality, bestiality, incest, and child sacrifice.[13] According to these extra-Biblical sources, this child sacrifice was about as heinous as you can imagine. Think *Indiana Jones and the Temple of Doom* kind of behavior, utilizing fire to burn their children alive.

If you've ever read through the Old Testament and scratched your head trying to figure out why God commanded so many of the specific sexual, dietary, or religious directives that He gave the people of Israel in their law, realize that many of them were in response to these depraved practices of the Canaanites. God knew that Israel would see the sick and twisted Canaanite rituals as they moved through the land, and He wanted to make sure Israel remained distinct and separate, not adopting any of the pagan behaviors.

Amidst all the depravity, it's important to remember that the righteous Abraham lived among the Canaanites, as did the virtuous high priest Melchizedek. Both of these men would have provided strong witnesses for God's will among the people of that land. And the Canaanites certainly could not plead ignorance when it came to God's seriousness, as they would have witnessed firsthand the destruction of Sodom and Gomorrah.

Furthermore, the conquering of Canaan happens gradually rather than all at once. Therefore, even after the first Canaanite city was taken by Israel, there would have been ample time for the remaining nations in Canaan to hear the news and head for the hills before Israel showed up on their doorstep. Consider the example of Rahab, the Canaanite prostitute, whose family was spared. Scripture tells us she had heard of what Israel did in Egypt, she had heard of what Israel had done to other Canaanite kingdoms, and she had heard of God's promise to Israel to take this land.[14] And it wasn't just Rahab who had heard. The pronoun she uses in that passage repeatedly is "We have heard." The Canaanites knew what was coming, but in a dangerous combination of pride, ignorance and arrogance, they ignored all the evidence of their impending destruction.

There's also one other significant point about the conquering of Canaan that we can't overlook. When we closely examine the language of God's commands to Israel, it becomes clear His interest is in moving the Canaanites off the land, not killing them. As Miller puts it, "Roughly, it was the 'nations' that were destroyed, it was the 'individuals' who were driven out."[15]

That conclusion is consistent with the language Scripture uses like, "But when you have driven them out and settled in their land."[16] In fact, if you add them up in the Bible, God commands "drive out" three times more often than He does "destroy" in these passages. The destruction only came for those Canaanites who would not heed and obey the ample warning.

The fleeing Canaanite families would be

absorbed by other surrounding nations and the evil Canaanite culture would cease to exist – precisely what God wanted. And remember that God granted plenty of time for this to take place. After they learned of what Israel had done in Egypt, the Canaanites had 40 years to pack up. And even after that, the conquest of Canaan took place step by step, allowing plenty of time for nations to learn from the mistakes of others and clear out. These were not surprise attacks from Israel – they were preannounced and easy to see coming.

By the way, as the genocide accusation crumbles around them, some skeptics will resort to their back-up argument that God is being "unfair" to the people of Canaan. They will point to the sins committed by Israel and ask why God held a double standard for them. The quick answer to that is: He didn't. When the Israelites began to practice the same rituals as the Canaanites – as the tribe of Judah did at one point – God expelled them from the land too, using the Babylonians to defeat and exile them. And if they didn't leave as they were commanded to, those Israelites were to be destroyed.[17] In other words, God was completely consistent in his standard of judgment.

So does this final example fit the Miller pattern? 1. It was certainly an act of judgment – but one actually intended as removal, not annihilation. 2. The crimes of the Canaanites were immense, grotesque and well known. 3. The destruction came after years of warning and calls to leave. And even then, God had numerous restrictions He placed on Israel when they attacked. 4. God was willing to spare the innocent – in fact, He was willing to spare them all if they would have left as commanded. 5. Children shared the fate of their parents (bad for some, good for others like Rahab's household). 6. The Canaanites who left when commanded, Rahab's family, and even the deceptive Gibeonites who tricked Israel into signing a treaty, were spared.[18]

So where does that leave us relative to the original accusation? In each of the four examples we have of this supposed complete massacre of innocent people – and remember, four examples is not many when you're talking about thousands of years – we see that the order was neither complete, nor a massacre. Each action was characterized by clear warnings, excessive patience, remarkable consistency, and benevolent mercy.

Far from being acts of genocidal mania, these were quite clearly acts of judgment for crimes, carried out in precisely the way we would expect a good, just, and merciful God to behave.

10

"LEAVING A LEGACY"

There arises a point in everyone's life where they become aware of their own mortality. For some, it's a near death experience like a car accident. For others it might be a devastating diagnosis from the doctor, the loss of a friend or sibling, or the increasing heat emanating from the surface of their birthday cake. For me, it was the quiet moments.

My life, like so many Americans, is incredibly hectic. My daily routine is a non-stop flurry of activity: teaching at school, driving straight to the radio station, doing the radio show, coming home for supper, running errands with the family or playing with the girls, putting the girls to bed, preparing for the next day's radio program, grading papers, and spending time with my wife before falling asleep. Throw in frequent speaking engagements, video projects or book writing, church obligations or activities, and there are very few moments left to catch my breath.

As a result, I don't have time to regularly dwell on the fact that I live my life as though it will go on forever. What I mean by that is that if I really thought my life might end today or tomorrow, I would probably reprioritize my routine. And while I understand you can't live every day like you are going to die the next second (people would get really tired of your outbursts of final words), it's important to regularly remind yourself what really matters.

That's what happened to me in those "quiet moments" I mentioned. Ever since my first year out of college, there will be random times I lay down at night and just become overwhelmed by realizing how short life is. I never used to think about those things, but I do now. And while the great unknown can be a bit freaky to sit and dwell on, I think it's an important exercise.

We find a lot of things to occupy our time. And there is great value in much of it. But nothing matters as much as what we do for the Kingdom of God, because when our days are up, it's the only thing that lasts. Many people work unbelievably hard to achieve great things here on this earth. And while some might do so simply for the temporal pleasures success can bring, the truth is that most do so hoping to leave some indelible mark on the world – to "make a difference."

But what ultimately makes a difference from the perspective of eternity? Does walking on the moon, or finding a cure to a human disease, or building a university? Don't get me wrong – I am NOT running down any of those accomplishments or suggesting that our human pursuits are worthless and lacking in value or purpose. I am simply demonstrating that with as great as those things are, and with as much honor as we should (and do) attach to them, there is still a greater calling and a higher purpose that every single one of us (not just those who have been gifted with particular abilities) can pursue. There is a greater legacy we can leave.

At my grandmother's funeral, my uncle Matt gave a eulogy that spoke to this very point. My Granny was a wonderful woman that I can still remember watching me play one man football in her backyard as a little boy. I would see her staring and smiling from the window as she watched the rampant imagination of a scrawny 8 year old boy transform himself into a star of the National Football League. Of course, knowing that I was being watched would make me extremely self-conscious about how silly I looked, so I would quickly wave her away from the window. She would comply, but it was only a matter of minutes before I'd look over and see her peeking out of another window in the house, this time with a camera.

I have so many great memories of Granny, but if I looked at it from someone else's perspective, there wasn't much in her life that others would term remarkable. She worked for years at Delco Electronics, was a good cook and a meticulous planner. But there certainly weren't any great achievements that would draw the attention of history books.

Yet Uncle Matt pointed out at the funeral that my Granny had three children, all of whom loved the Lord Jesus and were committed Christians. As a consequence of that, she had five grandchildren, every single one of whom loved the Lord Jesus and were committed Christians. As a consequence of that, she had seven (to date) great grandchildren who were all being raised in Christian homes to love the Lord Jesus. Uncle Matt poignantly observed, "Now *that* is a legacy."

Indeed it is. The kind of legacy that not many people can claim, and one that is far more enduring and far more lasting than others that are claimed. It's the kind of legacy I want to leave, and is the motivation behind a book like this.

Because while I hope that my meager efforts to address age-old questions will provide a renewed confidence in the faith for my fellow believers, I don't expect that they will be the final word, or will persuade great numbers of skeptics or scoffers to find the truth we all seek and the grace we all need.

While that may be the desire of my heart, all I can control is whether I am obedient to the command given to me in Scripture to, "Always be prepared to give an answer to everyone who asks you to give a reason for the hope that you have."[1]

These are some of those answers. May we as Christians always be prepared to give them...and in so doing, build a legacy worth leaving.

ENDNOTES

CHAPTER ONE
[1] Miller, Glenn. "A long-winded, heart-felt attempt to help a skeptic friend," published online at The Christian Think Tank: http://christianthinktank.com/sh0pre.html.
[2] The Holy Bible, Matthew 10:14.
[3] The Holy Bible, Matthew 7:6.
[4] Miller, Glenn. "To the person who just picked this up…" published online at The Christian Think Tank: http://christianthinktank.com/nextseat.html.
[5] Ibid.
[6] Ibid.
[7] Ibid.
[8] Ibid.
[9] Ham, Ken and Jason Lisle. "Is There Really a God?" *Answers in Genesis*, 2007.
[10] The Holy Bible, Psalm 14:1.

CHAPTER TWO
[1] Paley, William. *Natural Theology*, 1802.
[2] Atheist Think Tank, "Intelligent Design: Does it Prove God?" published online: http://www.atheistthinktank.net/articles/intelligent_design.html.
[3] The Holy Bible, Genesis 1:1.
[4] Ham, Ken and Jason Lisle. "Is There Really a God?" *Answers in Genesis*, 2007.
[5] Dawkins, Richard, "The Blind Watchmaker," W.W. Norton & Company, New York, 1987, 43.
[6] Ham, Lisle (2007).
[7] Spetner, Lee. "Not By Chance," The Judaica Press, Brooklyn, New York, 1997, 131-132.
[8] Gitt, Werner. "In the Beginning Was Information," Master Books, Green Forest, Arkansas, 2006, 127.
[9] Ham, Lisle (2007).
[10] Ibid.
[11] Ibid.
[12] Behe, Michael J. "Darwin's Black Box," The Free Press, New York, 1996, 252–253.
[13] Ham, Lisle (2007).
[1] Gitt, Werner. "In the Beginning Was Information," Master Books, Green Forest, Arkansas, 2006, 64.

[14] BBC News. "Professor's Alien Life 'Seed' Theory Claimed," February 1, 2010. Published online: http://news.bbc.co.uk/2/hi/uk_news/wales/south_east/8491398.stm.

[15] See SETI webpage "About Us" : http://www.seti.org/about-us

[16] Behe, Michael J. "Darwin's Black Box," The Free Press, New York, 1996, 243.

[17] Ham, Lisle (2007).

CHAPTER THREE

[1] Steering Committee on Science and Creationism, National Academy of Sciences, "Science and Creationism: A View from the National Academy of Sciences, Second Edition," 1999.

[2] Nye, Bill. "Creationism Is Not Appropriate for Children." Posted online at: http://youtu.be/gHbYJfwFgOU.

[3] Urey, Harold C. Quoted in *Christian Science Monitor*, January 4, 1962, pg.4.

[4] Jastrow, Robert. "A Scientist Caught Between Two Faiths," interviewed by Bill Durbin in *Christianity Today*. August 6, 1982, pg 15.

[5] Myers, Paul Z. Pharyngula blog, May 19, 2009.

[6] The Holy Bible, 2 Timothy 3:16.

CHAPTER FOUR

[1] "The Bible is Made Up" published online at Atheist Propaganda: http://www.atheistpropaganda.com/2008/09/bible-is-made-up.html.

[2] Miller, Glenn. "To the person who just picked this up..." published online at The Christian Think Tank: http://christianthinktank.com/nextseat.html.

[3] Ibid.

[4] Ibid.

[5] Lisle, Jason. "How Do We Know the Bible is True?" *Answers in Genesis*, 2011.

[6] Ibid.

[7] Ibid.

[8] Ibid.

[9] Ibid.

CHAPTER FIVE

[1] Barker, Dan. "Did Jesus Really Rise from the Dead?" 2003. Published online: http://ffrf.org/legacy/about/bybarker/rise.php.

[2] The Holy Bible, 1 Corinthians 15:7.

[3] The Holy Bible, 1 Corinthians 15:6.

[4] Yamauchi, Edwin M. Quoted in "Evidence for the Resurrection" by Josh McDowell, published online at: http://www.leaderu.com/everystudent/easter/articles/josh2.html.

[5] The Holy Bible, Acts 2:32.

[6] The Holy Bible, Acts 3:15.

[7] Strobel, Lee. *The Case for Christ*, Zondervan, 1998.

[8] Arnold, Thomas. Quoted in "Evidence for the Resurrection" by Josh McDowell, published online at:
http://www.leaderu.com/everystudent/easter/articles/josh2.html.

CHAPTER SIX

[1] Epicurus, 300 B.C. Greek philosopher published online:
http://freethinkingfordummies.com/2010/04/18/how-can-a-merciful-god-let-this-happen/.

[2] Smotherman, Christopher. Published online:
http://freethinkingfordummies.com/2010/04/18/how-can-a-merciful-god-let-this-happen/.

[3] Miller, Glenn. "Is God Cruel or Schozoid Really?" Published online at The Christian Think Tank: http://www.christian-thinktank.com/gutripper.html.

[4] Ibid.

[5] Linton, Irwin H. "A Lawyer Examines the Bible," Wilde: 1943, pg. 31.

[6] The Holy Bible, Romans 3:10-12.

[7] The Holy Bible, James 4:14.

[8] Chan, Francis. *Crazy Love*, David C. Cook: Colorado Springs, CO, 2008, pg. 42-43.

CHAPTER SEVEN

[1] Pock, Daniel. "The Bible: A Godly Book?" Published online at:
http://www.angelfire.com/fl/pointlesspage98/christianity/godlybook.html.

[2] Miller, Glenn. "Is God Cruel or Schozoid Really?" Published online at The Christian Think Tank: http://www.christian-thinktank.com/gutripper.html.

[3] The Holy Bible, 1 Corinthians 10:13.

[4] The Holy Bible, James 4:7.

[5] The Holy Bible, Genesis 1:26.

[6] The Holy Bible, Genesis 4:7.

[7] Miller, Glenn. "Is God Cruel or Schozoid Really?" Published online at The Christian Think Tank: http://www.christian-thinktank.com/gutripper.html.

[8] The Holy Bible, Jeremiah 31:30.

[9] The Holy Bible, Matthew 16:27.

[10] The Holy Bible, Revelation 20:12.

[11] Miller, Glenn. "Is God Cruel or Schozoid Really?" Published online at The Christian Think Tank: http://www.christian-thinktank.com/gutripper.html.

[12] Ibid.

[13] Ibid.

[14] The Holy Bible, Genesis 3:12.

[15] The Holy Bible, Genesis 3:13.

CHAPTER EIGHT

[1] Thiefe, Chris. "Slavery in the Bible," published online: http://www.evilbible.com/Slavery.htm.

[2] Dial, Karla. "Students Walk Out on Dan Savage," April 18, 2012. The relevant comments are posted online at: http://www.youtube.com/watch?feature=player_embedded&v=ao0k9qDsOvs#!.

[3] Miller, Glenn. "Does God Condone Slavery in the Bible?" Published online at The Christian Think Tank: http://christianthinktank.com/qnoslavent.html.

[4] Ibid.

[5] Ibid.

[6] Ibid.

[7] Ibid.

[8] Ibid.

[9] The Holy Bible, 1 Timothy 1:9-10.

[10] The Holy Bible, Ephesians 6:9.

[11] The Holy Bible, Colossians 4:1.

[12] The Holy Bible, Titus 2:9.

[13] The Holy Bible, Galatians 3:28.

[14] The Holy Bible, Colossians 3:11.

[15] The Holy Bible, 1 Corinthians 7:23.

[16] The Holy Bible, 1 Corinthians 7:21.

[17] The Holy Bible, Philemon 21.

[18] Miller, Glenn. "Does God Condone Slavery in the Bible?" Published online at The Christian Think Tank: http://christianthinktank.com/qnoslavent.html.

CHAPTER NINE

[1] Dawkins, Richard. *The God Delusion*, Great Britain: Bantam Press, 2006, 31.

[2] The Holy Bible, Deuteronomy 20: 16-17.

[3] The Holy Bible, Hebrews 13:8.

[4] Miller, Glenn. "How Could a God of Love Order the Massacre of the Canaanites?" 2000. Published online at The Christian Think Tank: http://christianthinktank.com/qamorite.html.

[5] The Holy Bible, Genesis 19: 4.

[6] Miller (2000), http://christianthinktank.com/qamorite.html.

[7] The Holy Bible, Genesis 6:5.

[8] Miller (2000), http://christianthinktank.com/qamorite.html.

[9] The Holy Bible, Deuteronomy 25: 17-18.

[10] The Holy Bible, 1 Samuel 15:5.

[11] Miller (2000), http://christianthinktank.com/qamorite.html.
[12] The Holy Bible, Genesis 15:16.
[13] Miller (2000), http://christianthinktank.com/qamorite.html.
[14] The Holy Bible, Joshua 2: 9-11.
[15] Miller (2000), http://christianthinktank.com/qamorite.html.
[16] The Holy Bible, Deuteronomy 12:29.
[17] The Holy Bible, Jeremiah 38:2.
[18] Miller (2000), http://christianthinktank.com/qamorite.html.

CHAPTER TEN
[1] The Holy Bible, 1 Peter 3:15.

Made in the USA
Charleston, SC
28 October 2012